The Secret Power of Paid Advertising

How Anyone (Including You!) Can Get the Attention of Millions with Social Media Marketing on Facebook, YouTube & Instagram to Explode Your Business in 2019

Written by Donald Nova

purposes only. All effort has been executed to present accurate, up to date, and reliable, complete information. No warranties of any kind are declared or implied. Readers acknowledge that the author is not engaging in the rendering of legal, financial, medical or professional advice. The content within this book has been derived from various sources. Please consult a licensed professional before attempting any techniques outlined in this book.

By reading this document, the reader agrees that under no circumstances is the author responsible for any losses, direct or indirect, which are incurred as a result of the use of information contained within this document, including, but not limited to, — errors, omissions, or inaccuracies.

Table of Contents

Introduction

Advertising is an integral part of marketing. And in the modern world, social media advertising is a must for all businesses.

Why is it so important?

For starters, the advertising world has experienced a huge shift regarding organic posts. In the past, advertising through organic content was free and the most effective marketing tool to reach a huge audience, but now, organic reach is down across most of the social media platforms. You cannot expect an ad to drive sales to your business by simply posting it on networks, and, thanks to clever algorithms, most of the organic content is lost.

Now, the mindset of social media advertising has been changed. Advertising has entered in a pay-to-play the game. This truth is hard to accept, but paid social media has turned out an effective tool for advertising campaigns.

Moreover, the boom in social media users has made the game tough, and it's getting tougher, so, if you want to play at social media networks, you have to pay. Paid advertising reaches more people, and, when used correctly, it builds new customer bases online, generates more brand awareness, leads video views, gets more users to your websites to make purchases, and much more.

But to some people, social media advertising is still just a buzzword that has no practical advantage and a complicated learning curve. Perhaps you are one of those people who still have doubts about paid advertising and whether you need it or not in the arena of your business. Or, perhaps you are someone who is thinking to harness the power of advertising of social media networks.

Social media advertising is the next big thing for brand awareness and promotion in 2019. 2019 is the time to embrace the change in the world of social media advertising and move with the tide.

It is clear that paid social media advertising is offering incredible advantages to business, so if your business doesn't use paid advertising, then you should go for it as soon as possible.

If this is your goal, then look no further, because this e-book is just for you.

This e-book focuses on advertising through three famous social media platforms – Facebook, Instagram, and YouTube. The reason for these three large social media sites is their diverse and huge number of users that are growing more every day.

This e-book will provide you

- Insights of the paid advertising on social media platforms,

- Their ins and outs,

- Testing tactics for your audience,

- How to get started with social media advertising,

- Developing an advert,

- Running and monitoring advertising campaigns, and

- Best practices and strategies to upscale your sales on social media networks.

A tip before you start your social media advertising journey:

The best advertising platform for your business will depend on its cost-effectiveness and reach to your target audience, popping up as many times as possible. Furthermore, the chosen advertising option should also reflect the right environment for your business to promote its products and services. Your right social media advertising platform can be one or all three.

Start from the beginning or choose your favorite platform to get started with social advertising.

Chapter 1: A Word on Social Media Marketing and Social Media Advertising

Advertisement, adverts, or ads, according to Wikipedia, are marketing communications for a promotion or to sell an idea, product, or service.

It is the action of calling target customers to something through paid announcements by an identified sponsor.

In other words, the advertisements are paid announcements of new products, services or programs, creating a need for products or services, drawing prospect customers to the business, and convincing customers that a service or product is the best.

In simple words, the presentation of a message to customers or prospective customers through any medium of possible media is an advertisement. The objective is to change the thinking pattern or buying pattern of target customers to generate sales by persuading them to take action desired by the advertiser.

Traditionally, advertising was only communication through mass media such as direct mail, newspapers, magazines, posters, television, hoardings, contests, and even people. Then mass media went through a revolution, all thanks to the power of the internet and digital media, and new media become a means for advertisement. The new media includes blogs, websites, text messages, and, last but not the least, social media. Based on the company's objectives, their target audiences, and budget, advertisers spread their desired messages through one or more types of these media. As mentioned before, the main purpose of the advertisement is marketing, therefore, along with the value or message of an ad, selection of an advertising media is really important to meet your business marketing goals successfully. Let's dive into some more details of different types of media for advertisements.

Print Media:

One of the traditional and most popular advertising types is print media. And why would it not be? Plenty of people don't start their days until they read their morning newspapers. For decades, advertisements through print media was a golden standard for advertisers and considered a credible and portable medium. Print media can be classified into

- Periodical Advertising

  Any print media is a periodical advertisement that comes out at regular intervals like a magazine or a newspaper. You can grab the attention by using a center spread ad of a bog magazine, its back cover, or that of a newspaper which can reach millions of people who see your ad and the message is delivered.

  Moreover, newspapers are available in the regional languages and within reach of everyone because of their economical prices. On the other hand, magazines are best for a certain niche, or reaching a limited or extremely targeted audience. Also, the digital presence has transformed print media, as most of the print media has a digital presence and is available in a virtual version.

- Point of Sale Advertising

  Flyers, leaflets, flyers, postcards, and handouts are point-of-sale advertising. It is everything that sits on a customer service desk, on a counter, glossy brochure, or small print media offer. These ads offer a more intimate way to engage the consumer and, hence, are treated as separate entities because they have less chances of being seen by the audience.

- Direct Mail Advertising

  Direct mail, just like it sounds, is sending printed advertisements directly to the consumer. Either of the print media mentioned above is send to mailers or to target customers to promote products, services, or deals. This interactive approach is direct marketing and also includes email and telemarketing. Direct mail has recently become more prominent because it allows direct engagement with the consumers and tracking their responses that can be used to measure return on investment and improve marketing strategy. But make sure that your direct mail is creative and intelligently executed or else it will end up as junk mail.

Broadcast Advertising:

Recently, broadcast advertising has become the most dominant way to reach millions of customers. Its effectiveness is unmatchable as a story can be better understood and can deliver its message more clearly if audio-visuals are used. The credit to this immense popularity solely goes to technology advancements for entertainment media like television, radio, etcetc.. However, this advertising medium is one of the costliest media, too. Broadcast advertising is categorized into

- Television advertisements:

  Television advertisements or commercials always have an edge over print ads because of their power to influence viewers' purchase decisions. They are best suited for creating awareness for a brand among the prospect customers. It is one of the most beneficial marketing investments for businesses but involves a lot of monetary investments and time. Television ads are divided between national and local time slots. Local time commercials are focused on selling products and services while commercials run on national time slots and offer products or services opportunities to reach the target demographic.

- Radio Advertisements:

  Spots commercials, or radio ads, are simple yet powerful messages to a target audience that may be interested in your offer, product, or service. Advertisers pay radio station for air time, and, in exchange, the radio station broadcasts the advertiser's commercial to its listening audience. Radio spots are straight read advertising messages in the form of jingles or multiple voices or sound effects. These commercials tell listeners where to find your products or business in an informative, serious, or funny way.

Outdoor Advertising:

Outdoor advertising, or out-of-home advertising, involves placing printed advertisements in locations that are most visited by the target audience. If used creatively at the right location, outdoor advertisements can prove to be the most effective advertising strategy for your product, service, or business. Outdoor advertisements can be

- Banners and hoardings,

- Transit ads like on buses, taxis, or other automobiles,

- Wraps

- Flags

- Events or sponsorship

Guerrilla Advertising:

Guerrilla advertising or marketing has become a prominent means for advertisements over the last 20 years. Guerrilla advertising, inspired by guerrilla warfare, is a form of irregular warfare used by armed civilians, and therefore strikes the targeted customer at a more personal and memorable manner. Therefore, it relies on unconventional marketing strategies for anything and hence, makes a valuable impression on consumers and yields maximum results. It is low cost and ideal for small businesses that need to reach a large group of the customer without breaking the bank. It is also effective for big companies for their grass-roots campaigns.

Digital Advertising:

Think of the latest website you visited. Did you see an ad there? That's an example of digital advertising. Digital or online advertising includes ads on the internet or other media devices like tablets, cellphones, Kindle, and Google home. Increased technology and research and developments in the digital world have made digital advertising the most effective tools through which advertisers can not only target their specific audiences through their advertisements at a low cost, but also can interact with them. Digitals ads are in the form of banner ads, text ads, pop up ads, etcetc.. These ads present an interactive message or an image on a publisher's website or a third-party website platform like Google Ads platform, formerly called as Google's Adwords, at a cheap cost.

Along with the internet, you can advertise digitally on social media sites. Businesses can send their ads on social media platforms to the users that would be most interested in their services or products. The company can use LinkedIn to reach millions of users by posting videos, their product offerings, and ads that can target to particular groups or demographics of LinkedIn users. Other social media sites, such as Facebook, Instagram, YouTube, Twitter, and Snapchat offer similar programs.

Why Paid Social Media Advertising?

Among all these media for advertising, social media remains a top marketing channel for business all over the globe. Whether you are looking for your existing customers, expanding your audience, engagement, or sales – the case of advertising on social media platforms has never been stronger. In 2018, the global digital ad spending on social media reached $58 billion, compared to $35.98 billion spent in 2017, and this number is set to grow in the future.

Setting up a business page on a social media platform and communicating to an audience on a global scale doesn't require any money. Impressions and influence on businesses were earned by organically, that is, posting unique and fascinating content. However, rapid growth in social media has led to sudden changes in its dynamics, which has made it harder for businesses to reach their target groups of the customers through organic content. As a result, businesses have started turning to paid advertisements on social media to get the audience they are looking for their sales.

Paid social media advertising is very different from the traditional form of advertising. It uses machine-learning algorithms and Big Data to find and reach your target audiences with ease. Each social media platform is designed to facilitate your business objectives such as website traffic, brand promotion, lead generation, sales, and more. You can even access the analytics for insight and enhance the performance of your social media advertising campaigns. Thus, paid advertising is the next necessary step in taking your sales to a new level of profitability.

Here are some powerful reasons to invest in paid social media ads in 2019.

Reason #1: Amplify Your Reach

Organic posting on social media is declining sharply because of constant use of algorithms. Moreover, the sheer volume of posts doesn't give you full control of the overall reach of your post.

The only way is through paid advertisements that give you a direct window to generate and drive more sales, leads, and website traffic. Also, you can make sure that your message is delivered to all your followers. It will increase your online visibility and give you a guarantee that your post has a place in the user's feed. Once you have a wide reach, you will have more opportunities for interactions and engagements with the audience.

With perfect and maximum impressions through paid ads, the audience will develop an inclination towards your business, and, when in need, they will go for your brand as a good solution.

Reason #2: Cost Effective

Cutting the advertisement budget is always on the mind of advertisers. And they are not wrong to make budgets their number 1 priority as conventional advertising channels are expensive. But advertising through social media is more effective and requires only a fraction of what your business used to pay.

Being cost-effective is such a huge advantage of social media advertising. Not only is social media advertising inexpensive, but you also don't have to spend much time creating it. It will take a few minutes, and some creative tools to create an ad at a low cost. If your advertising budget is tight, you can consider taking out loans for the advertising campaigns that will drive sales.

Reason #3: Target Advertising

Paid ads target a specific audience and allow you to reach relevant users who are interested in your brand and fit the demographics of your sales character. It will give you options to decide who will see your content on several demographic and psychographic factors. While organic posts could reach millions of audiences, you will absolutely have no control over who sees your ad, and it may reach the wrong audience. Also, once the user clicks on your ad, you can then retarget him, and, if this is done the right way, you can earn permanent customers.

Reason #4: Boost Brand Awareness

Considering that most people spend much of their time on social media, it is the best place to generate awareness of your brand. When your business constantly appears in the users' feeds, they will start recognizing you. The more your user will see your ad, even if they don't click on it, the more they will incline toward your brand. As a result, the credibility and purchasing behaviors for your brand will improve, and you will be able to drive more engagements with the users. And, when the time comes, your brand is likely to be their first considerations.

You need to make an effective and consistent plan for your social media ad. The plan can be to develop a habit to post insightful content, be it social or informative, and add a human touch. By doing this in the right way, you will be able to add new people to your network whom can become potential customers, and, in a short time, your brand will stand out.

Reason #5: Boost Brand Awareness

With the boom in the number of internet users and the advancement of technology, mobile devices have seen positive reception, and its use is rising exponentially. Research showed that more than 80% of the time people have spent on social media is spent on mobile devices.

As a marketer, you need to be right where your audience is if you want to maintain the impression of your business's worthwhile nature. Therefore, it is important to have an advertising campaign up and running on those social media platforms, which can gather more audiences and generate sales. In this way, when your customers intend to find you or make a purchase through their mobile apps, you are there for them.

Make sure your social media ad appeals to mobile users. Use minimal text and a strong image to communicate the value of your brand. Design your banner ad in such a way that it should blend well into a social media platform without making your business or brand look like it is invading your users' private spaces.

Content Marketing for Social Media Advertising

Here is a question for you. Are social media marketing and social media advertising the same?

Perhaps your answers is yes, like most of us, as its end result is the same. But you are wrong here.

Don't confuse marketing with advertising.

Yes, they do have similar end objectives – motivating the audience to purchase a product or sale.

But these two terms are distinct from each other, as each has its own process to reach their end objectives.

Marketing is a process of preparing your ideas, products, or services for a marketplace. It involves research and analysis to create a design for a product and then sharing it with the market you want. Therefore, marketing requires understanding the potential customers and need to only think of the benefits they could get from the product.

On the other hand, advertising will spread the word and make it known to the marketplace.

While advertising is how you communicate to the potential buyer the existence of a product, marketing is a way in which you persuade that buyer that it is the right product for them.

In today's smart world, generating sales is not just adopting an effective marketing strategy and running an advertising campaign. Do you know the content is equally important to build your business and help meeting its sales objective?

If you don't have quality content, your audience will not even spare a glance to your ad, and this will be a huge loss to all your efforts, time, and money, stamping your supposedly brilliant marketing strategy with a big FAIL.

So let's start from the root. Every marketing strategy starts with writing quality content, a content that sells. Before going straightaway into the selling part, first understand what the content actually is.

Content is anything that can be used to engage your audience – quality words, images, videos, or even sounds.

Content is blogging

The most common way to express yourself, your business, or your products is by blogging.

Blogging is not only an effective writing tool, but it can also be used to build your trust in the target audience. If you produce well-curated and quality content, the readers will consider you the expert in your niche.

Moreover, blogging can also help to increase the rank of your business in search. You can write a blog and then optimize it using search engine optimization (SEO), and then search engines will start showing your blog in their search results. If done correctly, blogging done with SEO will put your content in front of more eyes.

Some quick tips for efficient blogging – blog about the topic you know best or discuss new trends in your market. Come up with an engaging title to persuade your readers to give your blog a chance and keep holding their attention by using excellent content. Speak to your audience and provide information that is valuable to them.

Content is asking questions

Remember, through your ad, you want to engage

with your target audience. You want their response to know your followers better, and this can be done by asking questions. You can begin with asking a question on social media platforms and monitor the activity. Moreover, you have to regularly participate in the discussion and keep it active and insightful. People love to interact with the brand on a social media platform, and you have to use this for your business advantage. In this way, you will earn respect from your followers, and, in the future, when they will think of making a purchase, they will remember their online encounters with you.

Content is offering inspiration

Content writing doesn't have to always be about your brand, product, or service. Offer something more, like a little inspiration, that can benefit them as you develop your business. It shows that you care about your audience and want them to succeed in life.

Content is posting photos

You must have heard this a lot - images speak louder than words. True to this saying, indeed words aren't everything. Believe it or not, a photo is content because it says a lot about your product or brand. Therefore, never compromise on the quality of photos when posting on your social media accounts. The pictures need to be high-quality, sharp, and available in such a way that it should tell a story or be informative. Furthermore, you can also add a caption when you are trying to sell your product. Make your photos fun and exciting.

Content is video

Depending on your audience, you can play the content game by using video to deliver valuable content to your audience. The video should be as short as possible; a video length of 1-minute content always works. Investing time in curating content and shooting your video with precision are the signs of creating a strong video.

Now let's come to the selling part of your content. Your sales tactics need to be as strong as your content. You can go for:

Content is search engine optimization (SEO)

SEO, short for search engine optimization, is used to inform search engines that your website is best and should be on top results of their search results. This will drive traffic to your website, so, as soon you create a website, you need to optimize it as soon as possible. If your website is not optimized, then your potential customers won't see it, and you won't make any sales.

Search engine optimization includes on-page optimization like inserting trending keywords, titles, meta descriptions, and tagging images. Once you do this optimization appropriately, the search engine will get to know your website, rank it, and eventually, when a customer searches using your chosen keywords, your website will show up in the results. You can do SEO by yourself, and if your website rank doesn't improve, try asking for professional help.

Pay Per Click (PPC):

Pay per click (PPC) is a paid form of search engine marketing. PPC allows complete control of designing your advertisement along with setting its budget. The thing about pay per click is that, if customers click on your Google ad, they are already ready to convert, meaning customers will make a purchase. Therefore, if you have funds, you can utilize them in PPC, and, as a result, your business will show up as number one in Google's ad space every single time. However, if you want to do this without burning a hole in your pocket, you will need to search for appropriate keywords that relate to your business and build the advertisements. If you pull this through successfully, you will be rewarded by qualified leads/customers who are ready to purchase your product.

Social Media Advertising:

Social media advertising is a digital marketing tactic where you simply post your content on social media to market your brand. Social media advertising includes marketing through sponsored advertisements and remarketing. When you pay for your brand to market in the form of promoting its social media post, this is called sponsored advertisement. Sponsored advertisement makes sure that your potential customer sees your ad and converts. Remarketing advertisement helps to attract those customers who failed to convert after adding something to their cart or clicking on your advertisement.

Content marketing is nothing without digital marketing. When you create content, you can use digital marketing through social media platforms to distribute this content to convert customers. Integrating these marketing strategies and using them properly will boost your engagement and sales and will take your brand to the next level.

Timeline of Social Media Advertising:

19th Century:

- Thomas J. Barratt "the father of modern advertising" created a brilliant advertising campaign for the Pears Soup Company. It involves images, targeted slogans, and phrases, "Good morning, Have you used Pear's Soup." He introduced many interesting ideas to make an advertising campaign successful. Barratt constantly stressed the importance of a strong brand image and reevaluating the market as the marketing idea should hit the present taste.

- A French newspaper, La Presse, included paid advertising for the first time in its pages, allowing them to lower the cost of their newspapers. As a result, their readership extended, and profitability increased. Soon all titles copied this formula.

- In 1842, Volney B. Palmer brought a large space in various newspapers for advertisements at a discounted rate. The actual ad used to be prepared by the company wishing to advertise, and Palmer would sell them a space for their ad.

- In 1869, the advertising agency of N.W. Ayer & Son offered to create and execute complete advertising campaigns for its customers.

- By 1900, advertising was firmly established as a profession.

20th Century:

- The expansion of industrialization led to dramatically increased use in advertising. Industries wanted a substantial increase in consumer spending, and modern advertising contributed a lot to achieve this goal. This led to the development of mass marketing to influence the economic behavior of the population on a large scale.

- In 1925, advertising was promoted and declared as a vital force in national life.

- In 1929, Julius Klein stated advertising as the key to world prosperity

- The tobacco companies created new advertising techniques to create positive associations with smoking and, hence, became the major advertisers for selling cigarettes.

- In the 1920s, psychologists John B. Watson and Walter D. Scott tested advertisements with an applied psychology theory.

- In 1925, main advertisement media were newspapers, magazines, outdoor posters, and signs on streetcars.

- With the establishment of the first radio stations in the early 1920s, retailers and consumer goods started using radio to reach their potential consumers in their homes. The slogan, mascots, and jingles begin to appear on radio and then on television in the 1930s.

- By the 1930s, radio station owners started increasing their advertising revenue by selling airtime called advertising spots.

- By the 1940s, advertisers begin to understand the ways their consumers developed a relationship with their brands in a social and psychological sense. Furthermore, manufacturers started focusing on creating strong branded campaigns by using consumer and motivational research to gather more insights into consumer purchasing.

- In the 1950s, the DuMont Television Network introduced selling commercial television time to multiple sponsors.

- With the introduction of cable and satellite television in the 1980s, a new type of advertising showed up in the form of music videos, pioneered by MTV.

- Online advertising grew, a contribution of the dot-com boom in the 1990s.

21st Century:

- In the 21st century, search engine Google created personalized online advertising based on web browsing behavior of its users.

- Guerrilla marketing introduced unusual and unpredictable marketing approaches, such as staged marketing encounters of brands in public places, cars covered with brand messages, and interactive advertisements where consumers can become part of the advertising message.

- An increased trend came forward called embedded ads, such as advertising through text messages and utilizing social media networks like YouTube, Facebook, or Twitter.

- Registering domain names allow advertising companies to place advertisements on their websites or search engines like Yahoo and Google in return for generating revenues with per-click on ads.

Chapter 2: Importance of Social Media for Business in 2019

Did you know that 66 percent of all marketers that spend at least 8 hours on social media per week have generated more leads?

More than 90 percent of all marketers say marketing through social media has increased their business exposure.

No matter what you sell, be it a product or service, and who you sell it to, using social media platforms as a marketing tools can help you grow your business and pad your wallet. Here is what social media can do for your business in 2019.

1. Social media posts will drive targeted traffic.

   Whatever industry you belong to, a substantial portion of your audience, customers, or leads are on social media. A report "Social Media Use in 2018" by Pew

Research Center found that 68 percent of American adults use Facebook multiple times in a day. Even among Americans that are 65 years old or older, 37 percent are social media users. While 78 percent of users belonging to the age group between 18 to 24 years use Instagram, and 45 percent of users in this age group are on Twitter. Thus, young adults stand out in social media consumption.

Looking at these statistics, the research shows that having access to your audience through social media helps you boost traffic, particularly for a new website. So if you have created a new website and regularly post on your homepage, you need to post these updates on your social media as well. In this way, these posts will show up in your audience feed, and people that are interested in your product will remember you next time they search for the product that resembles your brand. It won't just boost your traffic, it will bring very targeted visitors you want to attract.

2. Social media improves the SEO of your website.

Through SEO, it has become very easy to find which webpages are consistently receiving more traffic and which are just floating out there and ignored. Of course, your effective content strategy is the most important factor in improving your search ranking, however driving traffic to your SEO optimized pages will cause them to climb these rankings much faster. You can easily achieve this by re-sharing your content, of course in addition to posting new content. Don't take this as a time-intensive task; you can plan every post to be re-shared with social media scheduling tools like Facebook's scheduling tool, Hootsuite for Twitter, regram for Instagram, and much more.

3. Social media helps you understand and learn from your audience.

Part of what makes social media channels the best marketing tools is the engagement you have with the customers. By reading their updates and comments, you will gain insights into their daily lives, consumer behavior, and psychology, enabling you to answer questions such as:

- What hobbies do they have?

- What websites do they visit?

- What types of posts do they love to share?

- What products are they buying and why?

- In what services they are interested?

These insights provide essential marketing benefits because, if you understand your customer, you can write a compelling post, which leads to more traffic. Furthermore, these benefits can help you identify your customers' main points, refine product strategy, and improve sales.

4. Social media builds relationships with your audience.

Social media, indeed, boosts your sales by bringing valuable traffic to your business page and converts them to purchasing your product. However, there is another side of social media as well where consumers see social media channels as nothing but a means of social networking, not marketing machines. Therefore, you have to be very careful in the interactions with your audience while developing your social media marketing strategy. You don't have to inundate your followers with discount offers, customer reviews new products, or service announcements. It will only bring in modest traffic to your business, and this shouldn't be your goal. You need to use your social media presence to transform your business, and this can only be done once you start seeing social as a way to connect them.

Remember that customers want authentic engagement through social media. You can help your audience by answering their queries, enlightening them with relevant content, notifying them with updates, entertaining them, and even forming new ties and bonds over shared interests. In this way, you will get a chance to build connections with influencers and industry leaders, and, over time, you will become more than a brand. This exposure brings in new leads, and, over time, these leads become followers, then followers convert into customers, and customers become brand promoters, and the cycle continues.

5. Social media advertisements allow targeting and retargeting.

Social media offers high targeted advertisements that can be easily customized as per your customers' needs. For example, Facebook ads target customers by factors like pages a user has liked, location, age, and even their education level. You can also track how your advertisements affect customer behavior and retarget your ads accordingly.

6. Social media is key to customer service.

Effective handling of complaints is becoming increasingly important in improving brand loyalty. Just like mentioned above, social media can prove more fruitful for your brand if used to connect with your customers. Encourage your customers to reach you out through social media if they need any information or have any problems regarding your product.

If you respond to your customers' query as soon as possible, it directly affects your profit because the businesses who value their customers the most are more likely to receive business. Therefore, a strong and active social media presence will help your customers happy and will keep your business image positive.

7. Social media will get you more sales.

The main reason your business needs to have a social media presence is to increase sales. Period.

Did you know more than 70 percent of marketers have acquired customers through Facebook?

Do you know CEOs and VPs use social media to make purchasing decisions?

When you stay informed of your customers, they are more likely to buy a product from you when they need it; but marketing through social media does far more than increase your brand presence. Social media marketing influences your target customer purchasing behavior at multiple points along the sales funnel such as targeting them with blog to aware customers about your business, answering customer question, addressing their pain points, or offering coupon codes.

8. Social media will find customers who don't know your brand.

Social media enables you to search and connect with customers who are looking for information related to your product. You can reach these people by running a search through keywords relating to your product or industry and then direct them to your website, or by explaining to them how your product is perfect to meet their needs. This strategy is also valuable for those customers who aren't familiar with your company. By reaching out to them with new information, you can not only influence their sales decisions, but you can also show them how your brand is growing bigger to address their needs.

9. Social media increases inbound traffic.

To be honest, without the social media presence of your business or brand, its inbound traffic is limited to people who are already familiar to it or people who are searching for keywords your website is currently ranked for. So social media provides another path that leads to your site and every piece of content. Thus, it is another opportunity to expose your valuable information to a new visitor. Therefore, the more you promote valuable content on social media, the more inbound traffic you will generate, and this means more leads and more conversions.

10. Social media decreases marketing costs.

Paid social media marketing doesn't have

to mean spending a huge chunk of money in the beginning. It is better to start small and give time to test for paid social media marketing strategies. In this way, you will also never have to worry about going over your marketing budget. Once you start getting results and get to know for what to expect, you can increase the budget and conversions correspondingly.

Your competitors are already on social media, which means your social media traffic and conversions are already taken. So don't let your competitors take all the advantages of social media marketing while you stand idly. The longer you wait, the more you have to lose. Even if your competitor is not on social media, then the field is completely open for you. The sooner you start, the sooner you reap the benefits, and the sooner you own it.

Social Media Trends That Will Matter Most in 2019

Trend #1 – Love Your Audience

Social media is all about engagements and relationships, and it is a two-way road. If you want your customers to be loyal to you or show love of your brand, then you need to shower your love on them as well.

In 2019, the top focus for business owners or marketers should be on being responsive to their followers. The thing about connecting and marketing through social media channels is about presence and interaction, instead of getting visibility or bringing traffic to your website. Social media will shift even more towards 1-to-1 interactions. No matter how large or small a brand is, every customer will expect more personal interaction.

In 2019, you need to be authentic when posting content and need to actively respond quickly to customer questions and their issues. You need to track, monitor, and participate in conversations with your existing and potential customers. In this way, you will be able to cultivate a more authentic relationship with your audience and will stand out among the high brands that don't.

Doing this with the right medium and in real time supports your stance that customers matter to your brand and you will be the winner in 2019 and beyond.

Trend #2 – Tell Authentic Stories

2019 is the year of authenticity on social media. These means your social media account need to create those stories that are raw, intimate, and offer transparency. The stories need to develop to form meaningful relationships between your customers and the brand.

But this also means more work on brands for advertisers and marketers for better storytelling.

To cut through the clutter, you need to share stories that matter to the audience, not your brand. You can even share secrets that matter to your followers. But how do you find the content that will matter to your audience?

You can start with the best content that have received more likes or interactions. Create one-minute videos on these topics and post them to your social media channel. Secondly, you can convert your best-performing social media post into an article. Sharing this article with your followers will boost your search ranking and traffic. In the same manner, you can repurpose podcasts and live videos into derivative content like articles, listicles, or articles.

Trend # 3 – Working with Influencers and Micro-Influencers

Connecting with influencers and micro-influencers should be a part of marketing campaigns in 2019. They are people that stand out within your community, people that others listen to and that create action. You can also use influencer marketing platforms like Traackr and Neorach to find big brands and develop relationships with micro-influencers at a scale which no human could match. Not only this, non-competitive influencers, business owners, and thought leaders can also be used for the promotion of your brand.

Remember, engaging to influencers in the right manner is the key. Before approaching an influencer, you should know who you are speaking to, when and how to speak, and when to shut up and listen.

Trend #4 – Video, Video, and Video

The trend of the video is nothing new. But in 2019, marketers, brands, and businesses must have video strategies in their social media marketing plans. The truth is that if a picture speaks a thousand words, then a video's worth is a million words. Plus, most people enjoy watching short and sweet videos instead of reading a normal text ad. Videos explain a lot about your business and brand and are always effective to engage lazy buyers. It is the best way to ask and speak to your audience and get to know what they want. Here's how you can use the power of video for your business in 2019.

Live Video: Social media users spend 3x more time watching live videos compared to pre-recorded videos. Streaming live videos is an interactive marketing tool to deliver content innovatively, enhance the user experience, increase engagement, and strengthen the product-consumer bond.

Vertical Video: 2019 will see more growth in vertical video consumption on social media channels, especially on Instagram and Facebook. If you want to preserve a memory of your brand success and want to revisit and re-enjoy in future, then this video marketing tool is a must-try.

Interactive Video: Video marketing is not just posting some native video on social media that your viewers can just play, pause or skip. A new way to create videos that will make your brand more memorable is to make it interactive. Interactive videos are the next frontier in video marketing in 2019 that will make your brand stand out in the sea of content. You will need to create short videos that can run as advertisements without seeming out of tune, and that excites your audience like integrating virtual reality or 360-degree content.

Video Remarketing: Video is remarketing increased conversion rates to 20 percent above normal remarketing ads. Choose your killer video ad, plan an effective remarketing strategy and execute it.

Trend #5 – Put Socialization Back in Social Media

Somewhere along the way, people have forgotten the true purpose of social media – socializing. Marketers, businesses, and brands have taken out "social" from "social media" for more than a decade now. Most people are using social media for creating brand awareness and driving traffic to their websites, failing to understand that their prospect audiences crave a sense of belonging and want to participate in meaningful communities. The result - business are losing their ethnicity and losing customers due to their artificial engagements. To foolproof your social media marketing strategy in 2019, you need to center social media around community socialization and offer authentic engagement that helps customers connect with you and create a meaningful relationship.

Trend #6 – Earn the trust, Rebuild it, and Repeat

In 2019, brands and businesses will need to work harder to capture and keep the trust of their target customers. With all the fake news, security breaches, and privacy disasters in 2018, audiences will heavily rely on brand messages on social media throughout 2019. This provides a golden opportunity for marketers by making emotional connections with target customers and keeping them loyal. Therefore, 2019 has no space for those social media marketing tactics that were misused and abused in 2018.

In 2019, you can regain the trust of your followers by increasing your paid advertising budgets. You also need to stop begging your audience for something all the time, instead engage them naturally with your content. In 2019, you need to stop selling and start communicating.

Advertising on Social Media

The number of businesses, brands, and entrepreneurs who implement social media marketing with online advertisements continues to rise in 2019. However, there are still some people who resist using social media advertising to increase their sales. This is more likely due to the fact they don't realize the advantage of social media advertising. Some of the most relevant reasons to go for social media advertising include:

Price

The expense of social media advertising is relatively low in comparison to traditional marketing techniques. Therefore, in 2019, businesses must dedicate a portion of their marketing budgets towards social media advertising, where you can easily achieve tremendous results without the skyrocketing cost.

Reach

Social media advertising allows businesses to reach a lot of people. This means you can reach a large number of prospect customers, potential clients and thus, an increase your conversion rate — the more, the merrier.

Segmentation

Social media advertising allows wide segmentation with respect to other marketing media. Therefore, if you are selling a very specific service or product, you can spread the word to specific users with demographic data such as sex, age, language, use of a specific website, education, socio-economic situation, and much more. These predetermined characteristics will allow you to search and identify your target prospects accurately.

Brand Visibility

To be honest, the entire world is on social media. Therefore, if a brand adds social media in their marketing tactics to advertise themselves and their business, their market visibility and brand awareness will increase considerably, which will lead to increased lead generation and conversions.

User Experience and Loyalty

Social media advertising is generally associated with a business or brand that has its own profile on a social media channel, and this creates a window for communication with potential clients. Therefore, a company can create a customer service account that will result in strengthening cooperative images of the brand in the eyes of the public while increasing sales of existing customers.

Connectivity

Social media advertising also serves as a tool to let a company create a channel specifically for customer interaction. This channel allows the clients to feel a sense of connection with a business. In this way, the new bond is established within the target audience and existent bonds strengthen.

Sales and Lead Generation

Social media advertising is an ideal way of getting more conversions, be it in the form of sales, leads, or website signups. If a user is given what they are seeking in an ad and they choose the right call-to-action, then advertising through social media is an effective method.

Creation and Knowledge of Prospect Audience

Social media advertising offers businesses a better way to understand their audiences, and, using that knowledge, can create new target audiences. Through segment ads, social media allows your desired clients to see your offer as much as possible. This same trait also allows you to establish a new customer who could end up becoming interested in your product in the future.

Social Media Advertising Myths

Online advertisements are not as complex as people make them out to be. Yes, some misunderstandings turn brands off of social media, but the reality is, when social media is used properly, it yields exciting success for the business of all shapes and sizes. After all, social media advertising holds immense potential in terms of reaching the target audiences and segmentations. So, here are five social media advertising myths you need to avoid in your 2019 efforts.

Myth #1 – Organic is best

Organic audience reaching has been on a decline for years. Furthermore, with recent changes to the algorithms on social media, organic audience reaching will remain low. In fact, in 2019 it is likely that only a single digit percentage of your social followers will see your organic posts. Still, some marketers still believe that posting organic content is more genuine and engaging than running ads and that online ads are a danger to the reputation of authenticity. On the contrary, paid social media advertising has brought real and enthusiastic engagement that is far higher in impact than content that doesn't get a paid push.

Myth #2 – Pay-Per-Click is too expensive

Money always comes first when it comes to promoting your business, and social media campaigns always take the first place for their low costs. It was very common to find inexperienced marketers turning to Adwords in the initial days of their social media marketing, and they often gave up after not seeing an immediate result. The reality is that paid social media takes time. You need to test your paid social media marketing strategy, monitor and measure your activity, and with time, you will see excellent results. Don't forget that online ads target those customers who are actively looking for a product or service, so they will surely engage with your ad.

Myth #3 – If my ad is not at the top then I am doing it wrong

This is a common misconception in paid social media advertising that paying for the ad means it has to be on top of page one, but this isn't the case. Conversion rates have no relation to the ad ranking. Your conversion rate will have just as good a chance in position #4 as it will in position #1.

Myth #4 – Social Media doesn't fit my marketing strategy

Keeping social media away and investing more time and money in the traditional marketing programs is a huge missed opportunity to make your business known and to gather the attention of interested leads. In 2019, companies and brands should go for lead generation and nurture it by content marketing, integrating with their paid digital promotions, and influence customers by paid social media strategies. For example, you can begin with the paid promotion of your high-value content on social media channels to capture leads. Automated emails, or chatbot, nurture those leads with related content to keep the engagement natural and strong while in parallel, remarketing content to the same prospect audience via paid social post.

Myth #5 – Social Media Manager can run paid social programs

A smart and enthusiastic social media manager that successfully drives engagements to your business or brand is definitely worth his weight in gold, but it doesn't mean that s/he can also run your paid social media advertising campaigns. Truth to be told, paid social media advertising is complex and is a specialized discipline, and social media advertising is no exception. Therefore, for your social media advertising campaigns in 2019, you need to a skilled and knowledgeable campaign manager that can understand your marketing needs and have a keen eye for how the paid social efforts fit into the big picture.

Myth #6 – Retargeting is creepy

Retargeting is an essential part of the social media advertising process. In fact, using demographic data of the users to target them with ads in a specific way is often described as creepy, and this puts marketers off from retargeting campaigns. To turn this situation into a blessing for your business, you need to carry out retargeting in the right way. Always try to deliver more relevant ads to your users through retargeting. If you set up an effective retargeting strategy, you will see conversion at a much lower cost.

Myth # 7 – Lead Generation ads are pointless

For most of the marketers, lead generation is an unnecessary step as they don't believe in spending more time and implementing those processes that will make the users click on their ads and persuade them to convert. On the contrary, lead generation plays a vital role in looking for an audience that converts. In fact, a large part of social media is about engaging your audience and prospect customers with valuable information through messages that generate leads and boost sales. Online ads are always ideal for lead generation campaigns and are the most effective way to drive conversions. Not only can these ads provide a chance to collect data from users who may be interested in your ad, but you can use this data to aid your converting these users with your product recommendations and guidance.

The Audience of Your Ads

Social media networking is all about connections without any middle men. If your social media ads aren't bringing you instantaneous feedback, and perhaps the reason could be that your ads aren't reaching the right people. Think again about who you need to connect and interact with on social media through your online ads. Who will be interested in your product or service? Does your ad lack uniqueness that could appeal to a specific audience?

Then think about the next level – who your audience might be associated with. Think about who these people can be, what they like, what motivates them, where they work, what their personality traits are, what technical know-how is, and how often they use social media.

Do your research on your audience and segment them by creating profiles. To develop a successful customer segmentation strategy, you need to ask these key questions.

1. Who do I want to talk to?

   - Potential customers

   - Lapsed customers (short-term, long term or seasonal)

2. What do I know about the customers?

- Name

- Age

- Gender

- Address

- Email address

- Phone number

- Income level

- Occupation

- Ethnic background

- Purchase history

- Profitability

3. Buying history of customers?

- Are they old customers?

- Are they occasional buyers?

- Are they big spenders?

- Are they specialist buyers?

4. Where do I hold this information?

5. How up-to-date is this information?

6. Does the information comply with data protection rules?

   Make yourself aware of data protection rules released by the information commissioner's office.

7. Are email addresses opt-in?

   Only people who have consented to receive marketing messages through emails should be included in the list.

8. Are the customers grouped into different types?

9. Are profiles developed for each type of customer?

10. Is my marketing communication targeted?

11. What are out conversion rates?

12. Are there some easy wins?

Dig a little deeper about your prospects. Think about following psychographics factors as well:

13. Personality

14. Attitudes

15. Interests

16. Hobbies

17. Values

18. Behaviors

19. Lifestyle

Keep a record of these questions in an excel sheet and make sure you review and update it on a regular basis to add more customers and keep up with the rules of social media. This data will help you determine how your product or service will fit into your target life to the T.

Moreover, you need to identify key influencers such as even peers, journalist and thought leaders, even stakeholders.

The audience you will be looking for include:

- Current customers

- Potential customers

- Associates of current or potential customers

- Affiliate businesses

- Journalist

- Editors

- Tough leaders

- Bloggers

Once you have decided your target audience, be sure to consider these questions.

- Is this enough to fit my criteria?

- Will my target prospect really benefit from my product or service?

- Do I understand what drives my audience

to make a decision?

- Are they easily accessible?

Defining your target audience is the hard part. It is an ongoing process and takes time. Once you know the people you are targeting, it will be easier for you to figure out what ads will resonate with them.

Copywriting for Social Media Ads

You now know all the background of social media marketing and social advertising but not how to go about writing an ad itself. If you want people to click on your ad, then you need to create content that your audience wants to see. In other words, you have to do effective copywriting for your ad.

Copywriting is content writing that sells, and a successful copywritten ad is the one that gets your customer to click on your ad and convert. Copywriting for social media advertisements is not what you say, it is how to say it. When you are copywriting for an ad, there are two key elements to remember:

1- Firstly, your advertisement reaches a targeted audience. The more specific your targeted audience it, the easier it is to write an ad.

2- Secondly, the copy of your ad needs to stop its viewer from scrolling. This can be done by a number of ways, but one way that always works is using an eye-catching image in your copy. Once you have selected an image(s) for your target audience, you can start to write your ad copy.

The next step is to write a headline (20 to 25 characters), then sub-headline, main text (90 characters), and lastly, insert a call-to-action button.

Headline – This should contain the most assertive or powerful words and keywords relevant to the people who should know about your product or service. Just like the newspaper headline, it must grab the prospect customer immediately and should convince him or her to go through the remaining ad as well.

Sub-headline – A sub-headline or secondary headline comes immediately after the headline and elaborates it. It informs the customer beyond the standard headline and reels the reader in.

Text – Text explains more about your product or service in simple, short, and compelling words. It talks about how your service or product can improve your customer's life and encourages the audience to take a certain action. It compels the reader to look, click, or do whatever it is you want them to do with your advertisement.

Call-To-Action: Copywriting finishes with a call-to-action. The text will bring your readers to a logical climax by enlightening them on what to do next, such as visiting your store or making a purchase. Without a call to action, your readers will be left wondering "what now?"

Here are some copywriting formulas that will energize your social media ads.

1. **4 C's**

   There are 4 c's in the world of copywriting. They are

   - Clear

   - Concise

   - Compelling

   - Credible

   If you can fuse these 4 c's in your social media ad, then you are on a roll. Start with the first C, clear – which means your copywriting needs to show clarity so that your audience knows what they are going to get. Conciseness means choosing the right length of your copy that aims to offer the right amount of information and persuasion that will make your reader click on the call-to-action button. Compelling describes your copy to be unique and incredibly eye-catching, and if your audience gets thoughts of good stuff after going through your ad, this means your copy is credible.

2. **The 4 U's**

There is another copywriting formula with 4 U's that means

- Useful

- Urgent

- Unique

- Ultra-Specific

You can use this formula to give an extra push to your prospective customers through your copy. This formula provides useful information in the copy that targets ultra-specific audiences. It has to be unique to beat the competition and should create an urgency, like your user should feel that if s/he didn't buy into what you are offering, s/he will suffer a huge loss.

3. **AIDA**

AIDA is the go-to for the most-used formula for copywriting at all levels because it works. This classic copywriting formula stands for

- Attention

- Interest

- Desire

- Action

Follow this formula to design your copy. Begin with grabbing the attention of customers with the headline and sub-headline, then tease them with interesting information and plant a seed of desire to learn more. Then tell the reader in clear words about the action you want him or her to take next.

4. **The 4 W's**

Your copywriting is a lot like telling a story but in a concise manner through the ad. You can write a compelling story for your ad by answering these questions.

- Who is this copy for?

- Why should your reader care?

- What can your reader get from it?

- What does your reader have to do next?

5. Add Cliffhangers to Make Readers Want More

Our brains are drawn to cliffhangers. We have to know what happens next, like what happens to damsel in distress; did the knight in shining armor saved her? Use this tactic in the copywriting of your social media advertising by ending your ad with a cliff hanger. In this way, your reader will be encouraged to click on the ad and go to your website to get that closure.

6. Use Social Proof

Inserting social proof to your ad is a sign of smart copywriting. Social proof means easing the minds of worried customers by adding certificates, product reviews, endorsements from experts and celebrities, and anything that adds authentication and value to your copy.

7. **So What?**

So what? This is a question on every customer's mind when he reads your ad. And before s/he can turn down your ad, you need to answer this question by getting your information in front of him or her.

You choose which formula feels best for you. Test these copywriting formulas until you feel good about what you are saying through your copy, and you will be far more likely to capture your reader's attention.

Advanced Tips to Nail Copywriting

1. **Do More Research**

Copywriting is nothing without research. You need to stuff your work with valuable information, and this requires plenty of work in the form of conducting tenacious research. Gather as much information as you can and then play with the words to write the best copy.

2. **Add More Interest**

When you don't know how to draft a better copy, or you're stuck at a point and don't know what to write next, there is one copywriting hint for you – add interest. However, this doesn't mean you can share some fake news with your users. A copy should always deliver the truth but in a fascinating way. Through your ad, you have one chance to grab a prospect customer attention, and you can't bore him into buying your product. You can only pique his interest into buying it. Here is how you can make your copy fascinating.

- Make it visually appealing and

scannable

- Add a unique selling proposition

- Make it entertaining and give it a touch of humor

- Incorporate controversy

- Tell stories

3. **Refine Headlines**

Remember the headline plays a major role in making your copywriting successful. An attention-grabbing headline should evoke a strong emotion, curiosity, or simply make your reader laugh. If your headline is weak, no matter how excellent rest of the copy is, no one is going to click on your ad. These tips will help you get started with writing a powerful headline.

- Write the text of your copy first and then use the strongest phrase to use as a headline. Make sure your headline matches your copy.

- The headline should be straightforward and simple rather than tricky or clever.

- Give readers a benefit and ensure you deliver it well through your copy.

- Paint a picture that entices your reader mind or stimulates an intense emotion to connect the reader with the product.

4. **Only Right Words Matter**

Simplicity is the key for an effective copywriting. Simplifying your content means making your message clear and concise so that your target audience understands what you are offering and gets the benefits as quickly as possible. So write the content of your copy simply and directly.

5. **Only Right Words Matter**

One of the oldest copywriting tips is to track down that very best word that conveys your message, imagery, or emotion. Right words make a difference; they make your copy stronger and it makes your reader see, feel, or understand what you want to say in a much better way.

6. **Give What Your Audience Wants**

You can't tell about yourself or your business in the copy. Instead, you have to focus on what your reader might be looking for or is interested to know. You can't create a desire for your product, but you can stroke and channel it. A great way to show that you are interested in your reader's needs and wants is by using 'you' instead of 'we' throughout the copy. Even using 'you' twice in a copy will get you great result in the form of more traffic, leads, and sales.

7. Make the Copy Visually Appealing

Make your ad copy inviting to look at it. If the ad doesn't entice the eye, no one will read it, it won't be shared, and it will get lost in the flood of online content. If you want your content to be eye appealing, then

- Use a good type of font that is big enough to read

- Add variation in the text example by bolding, italicizing, and underlining

- Use bulleted and numbered lists

- Write content in short paragraphs

- Indent quotes

- Use visual cues for call-to-actions, such as an arrow pointing to the button.

8. **Don't Be Clever**

Copywriting is a salesmanship of words, not clever wordsmithing. Using clear and concise words in your copy will give you more rewards than being clever.

9. **Make a Swipe File**

One of the effective ways to get yourself out when you are stuck on a tough copy or you don't know what to try next is by swipe filing. It is a file that contains a collection of great copies, emails, ads, and headlines that you love. Going through this collection will jump start your creativity at these distressful moments.

10. **Think Outside the Box**

Don't be afraid to try something new and different for your copy, because it just might work. Make a list of ideas for your copy and give yourself time to make the connection between them and that's when you will come up with your best copywriting ideas. Moreover, break the rules and speak directly to your customer, without caring about using proper grammar and syntax.

11. **Ask Questions**

A classic persuasion technique of copywriting is when you can get prospect customers to say yes. Once they say yes, they are more likely to say yes again. Throw a question in your copy here and there or phrase it as statements that get your readers to nod their heads. If they are nodding their heads and saying yes, then you have them hooked to your ad.

12. **Appeal to Emotion**

When writing a copy, think about the feelings and emotions that your readers might have and work with them in every possible way to get the best out for your copy. You can begin with asking yourself – what is my reader deepest desire right now?

13. Back up Your Claims

1- **You will build more trust and credibility through your copies if you back the information with reliable data. Support your benefits and other claims with valid proof. This wins over readers and shows that you know well what you are talking about. In your copy, you might include:**

- Facts

- Statistics

- Testimonials

- Methodologies

- Success stories

- Case studies

- Awards

- Media coverage

- Publications

14. Fundamentals of Persuasive Copywriting

2- Keep these fundamentals in mind while you write a write and revise. These copywriting essentials will help you create a stronger, compelling, and persuasive copy.

- Gains attention

- Focuses solely on customers

- Stresses on benefits

- Proves it case

- Establishes credibility

- Builds value

- Closes with a call-to-action

How to Set a Social Media Advertising Budget

Due to the rise of social media to boost business, it is common to see businesses and brands planning huge social media marketing budgets. It is even more common for these businesses to fail as well, as they don't have a proper social media marketing strategy. They are not sure of how much should be spent on social media marketing, on which social media channels and the right ways to get most out of their budgets. If you are one of these people or someone who is just getting started with a social media marketing budget, 2019 is the year for you to do it right.

Before talking about how to set your social media budget for 2019, it is important to have an overview of how creating a realistic social media budget can influence and pay off for your business.

Always start with setting a reasonable social media budget. In the initial days of your social media marketing, you are trying to find which social media marketing strategy works best for you. You might end up making some good decisions and some bad decisions. A reasonable social media budget will help you cover the losses of these bad marketing decisions, or those that don't generate the desired outcomes. It also helps to allocate scarce financial resources more effectively.

Moreover, a fair-minded social media budget makes you successful. If you know how much of the budget you can spend, you will have a better idea which marketing opportunities to pursue to amplify your marketing return on investment (ROI).

Of course, social media advertising is an important part and gives rise to so many bugging questions such as:

How much should I spend on social media

advertising?

How do I define my target audience?

What social media websites are best for advertising?

Can creativity impact cost and return on investments?

Should the budget be spent on video or image advertising?

How do I segment the budget for each activity in social media advertising?

How Much Should I Spend on Social Media Advertising?

Truth be told, a social media channel will ingest however much money you are willing to spend on it. The best way to find what will work for you is to look at your goals for 2019. The goals will define where you hope to go by the end of this year so you can find out what it will take to achieve these goals.

Do you want to generate 50 percent more engagement this year?

Do you want a 30 percent increase in your website traffic?

When you know where your business wants to go as a brand, you can plan the budget that will be fruitful for your social media advertising. Therefore, it is important to set your goals first, and that can be:

- **Community Building:**

    Social media channels like Facebook and Twitter allow their users to run campaigns that are just meant to create and grow communities. Therefore, its community building is important for your brand; you will have to divide your social media advertising budget to achieve this goal.

    If you have run these campaigns before for your business, then you must be aware of the cost per fellow, which can be determined by dividing the amount spent by the amount gained. For the future, divide an anticipated budget by the previous cost per fellow to get your new number of followers. For example:

Cost per fellow: Budget / followers gained = $100/250 = $0.4

New followers: Anticipated budget / cost per fellow = $250/$0.4 = 625 followers.

- **Generating Engagements:**

The more engagement you can create, the more people will know about your business or brand and the more awareness it will receive. It is highly recommended to always dedicate a portion of your social media advertising budget to promote your business or brand to a high targeted audience. Just don't leave your social media strategy for 2019 in the hands of feed algorithms. Take control and put some money behind your content.

The budget you will need in generating engagements for 2019 will depend on previous campaigns and its average cost per engagement. If you haven't done this before, this will be a little tricky, but not impossible. Gain performance data by testing a budget in the market, and, with reference to target engagements, determine the average cost per engagement. Multiply your average cost per engagement with the amount of engagement you are hoping to generate in 2019, and the result is the budget you needed to hit the mark. For example:

Average cost per engagement x target engagement = $0.25 x 1000 = $250 budget

- **Website Traffic:**

Using social media channels to generate traffic for your website is one of the most cost-effective ways to get new users. You will have to start with taking a look at your website average cost per click. Then multiply this cost by the amount of web traffic (target visits) you are hoping to get in 2019, the result is the amount of budget you need to nurture this goal. For example:

Average cost per click x website traffic = 0.8 x 30,000 = $24,000 budget.

What if you need to account for conversions, but your website visits aren't enough? For this, take a look at your website conversion rates in your analytics. You can then determine how much more traffic your website needs to trigger a certain amount of conversions. For example:

If your website receives 25,000 visits per month and has a 3% conversion rate, then the conversions are roughly 750.

Using the above formulas, you should get an idea of how much of your budget it should take to achieve your social media advertising budget for 2019.

How do I Define My Target Audience?

It is common to find businesses trying to appeal to everyone about their brands, products, or services. Keep in mind, everyone is not your potential customer, so targeting everyone in the circle is just a waste of precious time, a considerable amount of money, and your hard efforts. You need to determine your target audience. Once you discover who your targeted audience is, it will become easier for you to decide your social media advertising budget. Find out more about "The audience of your ads" in chapter 2.

What Social Media Websites Are Best for Advertising?

Knowing your audience not only helps you allocating budget, but it also helps you narrow down the best social network to connect with them. Rather than wasting resources and time to be active on every social media channel, you need to know which one your audience uses. In this way, you will save a considerate amount of money and will get a better return on investment from your target audience.

It will also help you to spend your budget wisely and efficiently for online advertising as the number of audiences that is unlikely to be interested in your offer is significantly reduced. Therefore, you should know the benefits of each social media platform. In 2018, Facebook, Twitter, Pinterest, Instagram, LinkedIn, and Snapchat were six distinctive social media advertising channels.

- **Facebook Advertising:**

  Facebook has become the largest social media platform in the world, hosting more than 2.2 billion active monthly users. It is concentrated with users between the ages of 25 and 54. Facebook is perfect for your social media advertising, thus making it excel at a lead generation with a cost below $1 per lead. You can post textual content like whitepapers, product coupons, limited-time offers, imagery, and videos.

- **Twitter Advertising:**

  Twitter is best for consistently evolving and fast-paced businesses, with 328 million monthly active users. It promotes organic engagement. Therefore, it exempts brands to pay to reach their target prospects. Twitter enables the users to update about their companies, share announcements, breaking news, brand awareness, and promoting specific products or services with direct conversations. You can post GIFs, videos, and textual content like articles.

- **Pinterest Advertising:**

Pinterest is a visual-based social media channel that was designed to find and purchase creative products. It has more than 175 million active monthly users, with 81 percent female users. Its highly-targeted search engine allows retailers to use Pinterest ads to promote their products and brands associated with their stores. Pinterest is perfect for any business, and according to Shopify, 85% of their users plan their purchases using Pinterest.

- **Instagram Advertising:**

Like Pinterest, Instagram is also a visual-based social media platform that has a younger audience. It has more than 500 million active users and commands in audience engagements that are 58 percent higher than Facebook and 2000 percent higher than Twitter. If your business belongs to industries like food, art, entertainment, cosmetics, and fashion, then Instagram will work well for you. The content type for Instagram is high-resolution images and videos, stories, and quotes.

- **LinkedIn Advertising:**

LinkedIn is a unique social media platform that revolves around business-to-business (B2B), offering high-end products and services, recruiters, and secondary education. LinkedIn excels at

B2B ads and social media marketing campaigns. It has 227 million monthly active users, and 61 percent of these users belong to the age group of 30 to 64. It is a great platform if you are looking for a high average disposable income. LinkedIn is also a place where you can find the highest quality leads, particularly in certain industries.

- **Snapchat Advertising:**

One of the newest social media platforms that is giving tough competition to Instagram and Pinterest is Snapchat. It has 301 million monthly active users, reaching 42 percent of all people that belong to the age group between 18 to 34 years in the United States. Though Snapchat advertising options are quite expensive, you can capitalize on its diverse features like augmented reality, filters, face swaps, and more to high engagement levels to promote your brand and boost its sales.

Can Creativity Impact Cost and Return on Investment?

You cannot use the traditional online advertising approach in 2019 by selling your product in newspaper style "Purchase, Purchase" promotion. You have to be creative on social media advertising. Your advertisement should be innovative and top notch that connects with the audience better, gains their trusts, and motivates them to give comments, likes, and share your ad. Your efforts and investments on your advertisement creativity will pay off over the long haul.

Should the Budget Be Spent on Video or Image Advertising?

Video and images hold equal importance in social media advertising, and in 2019, your social media marketing budget should have a portion for video advertisements. Even though creating high-quality videos is more challenging and expensive than a static image, they are incredibly useful. In 2018, businesses received more impact, more engagements, and almost three times more conversions with their video advertisements compared to still images. Thus, set up the ad by making a short and creative video that highlights the benefits the prospective customer will get from your product and service.

How do I Segment the Budget for Each Activity in Social Media Advertising?

While designing a social media marketing budget for advertising, you need to think radically and broad-mindedly so that you don't miss out on any aspects. You have to add everything in your social media activities lists, whether hiring a social media agency or a freelancer, arranging design and graphics tools for producing advertisements, outsourcing copywriting for your adverts or doing it on your own or monitoring the performance of your ads.

For example, you can allocate your budget to various activities in social media advertising such as,

- **Project management strategy – 10%**
- **Design and graphics – 15%**
- **Visuals and videography – 15%**
- **Ad spend – 40%**
- **Copywriting – 10%**
- **Monitoring and tracking results – 5%**

Creating a social media advertising budget and maximizing it can be a daunting task. However, it is fundamental to the success of your business. You have to frame a powerful social media advertising strategy, and this is done by analyzing continuously what you are doing; only then you will get most out of your budget and meet your advertising goals without losing much money.

Ways to Manage Social Media Advertising Campaigns

Now that you know the essentials of social media advertising, how to set up a budget, and what channels are available to reach your target audience, the next step is to decide how to manage your campaigns.

There are three primary ways to do so.

Manage Your Ad Campaigns Manually

The cheapest way to run an advertising campaign is to do yourself. There are no special requirements; you just have to head to the social media platform you wish to advertise on and set up your campaign.

It is ideal for those people who don't have money to hire an advertising agency. If this is your reality, then you will need to do advertising on social media by yourself. You can check out free online courses on EDX, Udemy, LinkedIn, or Coursera to get started with your social media advertising learning.

The Pros: Managing campaigns yourself allows you to devote 100 percent of your social media advertising budget towards testing ads and finding the winner. In this way, every cent goes directly into actual advertising. Furthermore, running your own campaigns provides you with a chance to develop your own marketing skills, which you can use to optimize ads in a better way and will persist in the future. Even if the tactics change, you will have a basic understanding of how things work for advertising on a given social media platform. So, if you are ready, enthusiastic, and willing to spend a significant amount of time to master advertising, this can be a great option for you, and if you succeed, your skills will bring in income for your business indefinitely.

The Cons: On the other hand, developing advertising expertise on your own takes time, they aren't developed overnight. You need to spend every hour in mastering advertising, and this is not a productive investment if you are a business manager or marketing manager because you are a supervisor and have the responsibility for other managing tasks. You probably can't afford to spend the time to learn and master social media advertising. Additionally, there is no guarantee that you will succeed in the end, and even if you do, it is very likely that your hourly rate for all the time is significantly more expensive than outsourcing advertising to get guaranteed results. It is a massive gamble with speculative upsides and guaranteed downsides.

Manage Your Ad Campaigns with Automated Software

The social media industry is filled with third-party tools. The tools are actually software that are developed to assist agencies, entrepreneurs, business owners, and in-house teams to achieve advertising success without much effort. If you don't have time to run social media advertising manually, or you don't have enough budget to hire an agency, then third-party tools are ideal for you.

The Pros: There are on-site advertisement managers that optimize campaigns, but they aren't always user-friendly. Tools like Adespresso can work as a great alternative to optimize your ad campaigns for a certain platform along with analyzing their results. There are other tools that make use of artificial intelligence to automate entire ad campaigns, thus allowing you to keep tabs without doing much. The social media industry has hundreds of different tools which perform at a high levels and saves the time you have to spend manually to master, manage, and monitor your ad campaigns.

The Cons: Great tools always comes with a great price and social media tools have no exception. Though social media marketing tools for advertising come up with a relatively affordable price, they are an additional expense in the budget that you have to take into consideration. Plus, there is no guarantee the tools will give the desired results or improve your results. And the worst part, it is not simple to identify where the tool is underperforming, and you might be clueless at how to troubleshoot the problem in your social media advertising strategy.

Hire an agency to run your ad campaigns

The simplest, the most successful but the most expensive option to run your social media ad campaign is to hire professional. By hiring a professional social ad service, you can accelerate the guesswork, and you don't have to worry about the hurdles that come with DIY social media advertising. Simply let experts handle advertising for you. A hired social advertising service will thrive your business with guaranteed profitable ad campaigns that will pour in sales from day one. If you have a grand social media marketing budget and need immediate results, then paid social advertising run by experts is your way to go. You never need to question about whether ad campaign is working, their performance, or the exact return on invest (ROI) they will provide. And still, even if your business is not progressing, you know exactly who is at fault. You can fire the agency running your ad and can go for selecting a new and better agency.

The Pros: Hiring a professional advertising team will give really good results, without any work on your part. You get to keep focusing on doing what you do best, leaving a marketing team to take care of the entire advertising process for you. Imagine, what can be better than consistent sales and new customers without doing anything, almost for free.

The Cons: The only downside to hiring an advertising agency is that you can't be sure if the agency is really an expert in this field. There are thousands of advertising experts who are only proficient in convincing clients to waste money on them, and as a result, you can end up losing a lot of money. Before you hire professional help, run a background check on the agency, explore their client portfolio and previous advertising projects, and pay attention to details. Even if this is not enough, you can also conduct a paid test to test their skills.

Donald Nova

Chapter 3: Advertising with Facebook

There is no doubt that social media is an ever-changing landscape and its rules change constantly. In the beginning, only having a presence on Google was enough. Then Facebook became king of social media in the 2000s, and, as the technology evolved, it gave tough competition to its fellow social media platforms - YouTube, Twitter, and LinkedIn. Now, Instagram, Pinterest, LinkedIn, and Snapchat are taking the world of social media by storm. And this is not the end. Yahoo, Tumblr, WhatsApp, Wechat, and other social media platforms are also in line.

But which one is the best for my business in 2019?

That's a difficult question, and, sadly, there is no right answer. Each of these social media platforms has their own weaknesses and strengths.

However, marketing experts and business owners have found that focusing on the big three – Facebook, Instagram, and YouTube – can bring your business in front of lots of eyes in 2019 without spreading your social media advertising budget too thin.

Let's begin with the key social media advertising platform in 2019 – Facebook.

As of November 2018, more than 2.2 million users have become part of the Facebook community. Its huge, global audience makes Facebook fit to promote any business, be it for teens, adults, or seniors. But frequent changes in the Facebook algorithm make this platform a challenge to gather conversions for a business organically. That's where paid Facebook ads come in.

In 2018, it was found that 93 percent of social media marketers prefer Facebook for their advertising campaigns.

Facebook ads use micro-targeting to reach the

exact target audience that buys your product and become converts on a long-term basis. Using features of micro-targeting, the Facebook ads bring your message in front of those people who are most likely to buy your product or service, simply by using demographic characteristics of the audience such as location, interests, profitability, and much more as explained in chapter 2 under the heading "The Audience of Ads."

Facebook Advertising Strategy for 2019

Facebook clearly knows that the future of all brands lies in social media advertising, and it seems very dedicated to making this process transparent, simple, and easy to manage for the business of all scales. Facebook advertising will look a little different in 2019. Here's what you need to know to plan your Facebook advertising strategy for 2019.

Facebook Ads 2019: Building Audience Segments

The most effective method for finding an audience has always been keywords, but in 2019, that won't be the case. Targeting an audience by using detailed audience data is a much better method to get qualified users interested in your product quickly. It means that segmenting an audience is a crucial part of any 2019 social media marketing strategy. This can be done just like you might segment your email list into groups such as demographics, interests, behavior, etc.; you need to perform audience segmentation to target audiences on Facebook in the same manner. With each segment, you can craft better copies for your ads that can resonate a certain interest in your user.

Facebook Ads 2019: Embrace Automation

In 2019, Facebook will be replacing a lot of manual and mundane tasks with automation. It has already started with introducing new ad categories like dynamic ads, where advertisers can upload their entire product line or service catalogs, set their campaigning time, and leave the rest of the advertising work for Facebook. Moreover, working with the Facebook Pixel will automatically show ads of the right product to its users.

Facebook Ads 2019: Facebook Stories Ads and AR Ads

In 2019, Facebook will reveal a number of incredible visual features that will take video advertisements to the next level. Facebook has introduced and heavily promoted Facebook stories ads, and, just like Snapchat and Instagram, it will definitely create a major impact on sales and Facebook as a whole. Also new to Facebook are the augmented reality ads that allow users to interact with their products virtually, such as the "tap to try on" option on a makeup ad. These new ad features are going to make Facebook advertising fun.

Facebook Ads 2019: Emphasize on planning with Creative Compass

Facebook has provided a solution to marketers in the ever-present challenge to understand a user's journey and the overall impact of an advertisement before it hits the market. To provide these performance insights, Facebook has introduced its new tool "Creative Compass." Creative Compass measure multiple key factors like noticeability, brand fitness, visual impact, and more advanced factors. It is already in the testing phase and is expected to release sometime next year.

Factors to Determine the Cost of Facebook Ads

Your Bid

When you send your ad in the global market of Facebook, you are competing with other advertisers for ad space on Facebook. So how do you win this competition? The answer lies within your bid; it shows how much interest you have to show your ads to Facebook users. If your Facebook ad bit is too low, then your ad may not get their deserved exposure, and you will not meet your marketing objective. This doesn't mean that your bid amount should be a high amount. With a high bidding amount, your ad can still end up paying the lowest possible amount to be delivered to the target audience.

Relevance and Quality of Ad

Facebook analyzes your ad performance on its quality and relevancy. It considers both positive feedback, such as a number of clicks or installations, and negative feedback, such as users ignoring your ad by clicking on the little cross on the ad. If your advert relevance score metric in Facebook ads manager is high, Facebook will show your ad more to the audience than the ads with lower scores, and, in this way, you will pay less to bring your ad to the target audience.

Estimated Action Rates

Before showing your ad to the target audience, Facebook firstly estimates how likely a user will act on your ad; this is called estimated action rate. If the estimation is low, then your ad rates will get higher ratings. To make sure your ad is shown to your target audience, keep your budget and bid high enough to get a few results per day.

Target Audience

The cost of a Facebook advert is highly influenced by its target audience and size. There is a lot of competition in the digital world; every day the number of marketers that seek to reach a specific target audience is increasing, and it makes the process more expensive to reach them.

Time of the Year

When the number of advertisers increase, so does the cost of ads. There are peak times in the years when advertisers and Facebook ads increase exponentially. During these times, there will be more competition, and, as a result, you will have to pay more to reach your specific target audience. So, if you are planning to run your Facebook ad campaigns around peak times or big events of the year, it is important to plan your ad budget according to the competition.

Facebook Pixel: A Key tool for Facebook Lead Generation

Before rushing to Facebook Ad manager to create your advertising campaign, I have a question for you.

Do people know that your business is on Facebook?

If yes, then you can go ahead, but if your answer is no, then you must stop and focus on building an audience. One of the cheapest, simplest, and easiest ways to bring the audience to your Facebook business page is by attracting your existing website traffic to it. So, if you have a website that is already frequently trafficked, then you should take advantage of this opportunity to promote your Facebook page. And, installing Facebook Pixel can help you with this task.

Facebook Pixel is an essential tool that brings the audience to your Facebook business page and simultaneously gets the audience to become leads that convert. It is a code that you place on your website, and, when it runs, it triggers first-party and third-party cookies to track your users as they interact with your site. You can then use the collected data by Facebook Pixel to create Facebook ads, either from scratch or you can improve your previous ads that target your audience in a much better way. Furthermore, Facebook Pixel also helps with optimizing your Facebook ads, tracking their conversions, and remarketing to the audiences who have already made a purchase or have taken some action on your website. Overall, Facebook Pixel's increase return on investment (ROI) improves your Facebook advertisement conversions.

Facebook Pixel offers the following seventeen different event codes to copy and paste on your website.

1- Purchase – making a purchase of a product or service on your website.

2- Lead – signing up or identifying as a lead on your website.

3- Complete registration – completing a form like registration or a subscription form on your website.

4- Add payment info – sharing payment information during the purchasing process on your website.

5- Add to cart – adding a product to their shopping cart on your website.

6- Add to wishlist – adding a product to a wish list on your website.

7- Initiate checkout – starting the checkout process to purchase something on your website.

8- Search – using the search option to look for something on your website.

9- View content – landing on a specific webpage on your website.

10- Contact – contacting your business.

11- Customize product – selecting a specific version of a product, like choosing a certain shape or color.

12- Donate – donating to a cause on your website.

13- Find a location – searching for the physical location of your business.

14- Schedule – booking a business appointment.

15- Start trial – starting a free trial of your product or service.

16- Submit an application – applying for your product or service like a credit card.

17- Subscribe – subscribing to a paid product or service.

You also have an option to customize events based on URL rules or keywords. The custom event gathers more details which standard events cannot provide.

How to Add the Facebook Pixel to Your Website

Now that you know why Facebook Pixel is important for your Facebook ads, it is time to create your Pixel and add to your website.

Step # 1: Create Facebook Pixel

Go   to https://www.facebook.com/events_manager and log into your Facebook business account. You will see three options of Facebook event managers. These are Facebook Pixel, offline events, and app events. You have to select "Facebook Pixel: Track Website Activities" and begin working with Facebook Pixel by clicking on "get started."

A box will appear where you need to type your Pixel name and website URL. The name your Pixel uses will create words that relate your business rather than your ad campaign. Also, keep in mind that an ad account can only get one Pixel. When done, click on create.

Next, you have to choose a method to add the Pixel code to your website.

If you have an e-commerce platform like Google Tag manager or Shopify, you can easily install Facebook Pixel by connecting to your platform.

You can also have your Facebook Pixel code mailed to your developer.

Another way to install Pixel is to edit the header code of your website directly and to paste your Facebook Pixel code. Your Facebook Pixel code looks like this:

Scroll through this page and turn on automatically advanced matching. This feature will match the hashed data of your audience from the website with their Facebook user profiles.

In the last step, you have to type your website URL to send your web traffic to your Pixel and then click "Send Test Traffic." Wait for a while until the Pixel code is active and begin receiving traffic.

Click on continue to move ahead.

Step #3: Select events for your business

First, select the appropriate category to which your business belongs. You have nine options that are automotive, e-commerce and retail, education, entertainment and media, financial services, professional services, real estate, technology, or travel.

Then move on to select events. Most of the events are turned on by default, therefore, first turn on the events that are necessary for your Pixel and then extend your desired events to input values in the parameters, if required. Some events will just require copy and paste of event codes.

Click on done when you have finalized the events.

If you want to use the custom event for your Facebook Pixel, go to https://www.facebook.com/events_manager, click on custom conversions on the top menu, and then click on create custom conversion on the bottom of the page.

Define your audience with URL rules. Add a name, category, and value, and when done, click on create.

Facebook Sales Funnel

Facebook ads are not very expensive, and they bring more conversion rates and returns on investment (ROI) when done in the right way. And the right way is to have a Facebook sales funnel in place.

So what is a Facebook sales funnel?

Facebook has huge selling power, but it is nothing without a sales funnel. A Facebook sales funnel generates demand for a product or service by reminding the Facebook user about needs that they didn't know they had.

Sales funnels capture and boost your users' interest by using relevant messages, and advertisements are the perfect medium to deliver these messages. The idea behind the messages is to make your audience consider the offer at different stages for purchasing your product or service and then slowly prod them to convert.

The stages of Facebook sales funnel are:

Awareness Stage

Your users first discover your product or service and are first made aware of it. Users at this stage may not even realize that they need a product, so they are obviously not ready to make a purchase. Instead, at this stage of the sales funnel, your goal is to grab attention so that you can follow up when your potential customer is ready to consider your product. Your job is not done just by telling the targeted audience to do this once. No, you have to do this on a regular basis and on a personal level to build a strong connection.

Consideration Stage

Once users have identified that they have a need for your product, they are interested in it and may consider its purchase in the future. The timing is now perfect to reach your customer again through the ad and subtly introduce your calls-to-action. If you succeed in providing something valuable and interesting, you will generate a lead for your business.

Decision Stage

At this stage, users are at the purchase stage of your sales funnel and are considering your product or service to be the best option. They are seriously considering purchasing your product or service starting with your moderate price, free trial offers, and other ways to get started with the purchasing process.

Retaining Stage

Users have purchased your product, but you shouldn't forget about them; you need to keep engaging and pursuing your users to take your calls to action.. In this way, you will turn your one-time customer into a long-time one.

And go back to stage 1.

All people go through these sales stages at various times and at various speed. If you use these stages as a model to create your Facebook advertising strategy, you will end up a winner.

Now apply these stages to your sales funnel for your Facebook ads.

Step # 1 – Generate Awareness

Your potential customers can't move through your sales funnel until they are aware of it and in it. To can generate awareness using several strategies such as,

- Targeting specific users through your Facebook ads that are interested in your product or service. Make sure they are not connected to your Facebook page. These Facebook ads should provide a quick introduction to your product and why your customer needs it.

- Gathering leads through the sales funnel by running a referral contest. Plan a social media contest and offer users something exciting if they refer a friend or family member to sign up into the contest. Once they do, you have the contact information of your user and their referral which you can use for your retargeting ad campaigns.

Step # 2 – Appeal to Pain Points

Through your sales funnel, you need to prove to your potential user that their life is incomplete without your product or service. This means highlighting your user's needs, their pain points, and simultaneously overcome any objections may have. You can do this by:

- Running retargeting ad campaigns on potential users that have expressed their interest in your brand. You can target viewers of your video advertisements or the audience who visited your website.

- Answering all comments on your advertisements. Everyone likes attention, especially the ones who are in the mood of purchase. These people are looking not just to decide if the product is worth the money, but they also need to know if it is worth the time as well or not. And this is your chance to overcome or fight the objection(s) the user has mentioned through their comments on the ad.

- Using a combination of ads and organic posts to remind your potential customers about your product's specific features and benefits and why they need them.

Step # 3 – Offer immediate Incentive

You need to give a little nudge to your potential customers who are lingering at the edge of the purchasing stage of your sales funnel. You can do this by:

- Running ads with special discounts or 10 percent off on their first order. You can also offer free shipping or in the form of flash sales like "only 6 hours left!" These messages in the ads create urgency while simultaneously offer incentives that your potential customer can't ignore and will lead him to convert.

- Running targeted advertisements on custom audiences from your website.

Step # 4 – Encourage repeat purchases

Making a customer convert and purchase your product isn't the end; there is still so much to do. Of course, you can move on to the new customer, but you must not forget the previous or first-time customers, you have to keep them engaged, too.

If you approach your existing customer with a new offer, they will definitely go for the purchase because they have developed trust with you through their previous purchase(s). You should use this trust and satisfaction level to drive further purchases, even with a higher purchase value. Strategies that can help you with repeat purchases include:

- Using purchase history to run ad campaigns and targeting customers with complementary products that will go well with what they have bought in the past.

- Using carousel ads to show variation between different products with their features and price differences to increase the purchase value.

- Using retargeting ads to reach high-value customers offering special perks like free shipping or special discounts.

- Running a referral program through your ads and pursue your customer for more purchases with discounts or other incentives if they bring new clients to you. You can also ask for reviews which you can use as social proof in your ads and will help you sell your product or service better than others.

How to Advertise on Facebook

Before heading to the Facebook Ads Manager, your business must have a Facebook page, only then you can set up a Facebook ad campaign.

If you don't have a Facebook business page,

follow these steps to create one.

1- Go to facebook.com/business, click on the drop-down menu on the right-hand corner and click on create a page.

2- Then log into the Facebook account. You will be present with two options – business or brand, or community or public figure. Click on get started button under the heading of "business or brand" and a box will open that will ask for more details. Type the name of page and category that your customer is most likely to come up when they think about your business. You can select the category from the list of potential category options. When done, click on continue.

Accept Facebook terms and conditions for Business pages and proceed forward.

3- Upload cover image and profile picture for your Facebook business page. The images should be visually good, well shot and prominent so that customers could easily identify your business or brand through these images. The safe bet is to use the company logo in the profile picture as it will appear in Facebook search results, or when you will interact with customers.

Now, your business page is alive.

4- Explore your business page or click through the prompts to know how your page operates.

5- You will be required to write a short description based on a couple of sentences to describe your business or its product(s). Use powerful words in the description to grab customer attention.

6- Click on "Create a Username for your page," and a box will pop up where you can type your page username. Username of a Facebook page ensures people can easily find your page in search. Make it unique, memorable and easy to type.

When you are done, click on "Create Username."

7- Add more details about your business page in the "About" section. Here, you can edit general information of your business, edit business and contact info. The about section is also a great place to share detailed description of what your business or product is offering to your customer through a story.

8- Last but not least, before you start inviting the audience to visit your page, you need to add valuable content to your page. Create some compelling posts, share relevant content in your industry or post something inspirational or motivational. You can also use the status box to create a post for a product offer, adding a milestone and much more. Just make sure your post offer value to your customers in a clear and concise manner. With all this, you are ready to engage your target audience with your business.

Now, head over to Facebook Ads manager to create your ad campaign.

Step # 1 – Know your objective.

Access to Facebook Ad manager tool through this link: https://www.facebook.com/adsmanager; log in with your Facebook business account details and then click on "create" box in green color on the left side of the page.

A box will appear where you will be given two ways to get started with a campaign – guided or quick creation. Then you will be asked to select a marketing objective from any of the three clusters:

Awareness

- Brand awareness – introduce, boost and promote your product or service to a new audience.

- Reach – provide exposure to your product

or service to as many potential customers as possible.

Consideration

- Traffic – drive targeted audiences to a specific page or website.

- Engagement – reach your audience on a wide scale to increase likes on your pages and convince them to take advantage of your business offers.

- App installs – pursue people to install your app.

- Video Views – get more people to watch your video.

- Lead Generation – grow prospect customer into your sales funnel.

- Messages – communicating your customers via Facebook messenger.

Conversion

- Conversions – convince the target audience to take a specific action like buying your product, use your service, like your page or subscribe to your list. It also increases engagement and conversions on your website.

- Catalog Sales – connect your product catalog with Facebook ads for those people who are interested in buying your products.

- Store Visits – Drive potential customers to stores.

The next steps for creating a Facebook ad campaign will be based on your selected marketing object. Here I am going to choose "engagement" as my campaign objective.

Step # 2 – Name your ad campaign

Scroll down the campaign page to type the relevant name of your campaign. You will then choose to turn on the split test and budget optimization.

Split A/B Test: provide insights for your social marketing plan by allowing you to test small details of your marketing material to determine which is most effective to meet your campaign goal and reach the audience most effectively.

Budget Optimization: Turn on this option if you are using multiple ad sets, otherwise leave it off.

To continue building your campaign, click on "Set up Ad Account."

Step # 3 – Ad Account

Set up your ad account in this window. Enter your country in "Account Country," preferred currency and time zone. When you are done with setting your ad account, click on continue.

If you already have set up an account, you won't be seeing this form.

Step # 4 – Reach your audience

In the "Ad Set Name" space, write a customized

name using ad set or campaign information.

Scroll this page to start building your target audience, ad placements, setting budget and advertisement schedule.

Custom Audience: In the audience block, you will see space to add information about the custom audience – people who already know your business, have interacted with your product or service, newsletter subscribers or your customer lists. When you upload this custom audience information, Facebook will process it and find matches with Facebook profile.

Another way to generate a custom audience is through your website by installing Facebook Pixel. The Facebook Pixel can match your website audience to their Facebook user profiles and hence, you can use that data to create a list of the custom audience for your Facebook advertising.

Locations, age, gender, and languages: Select locations as many as you want, age group, gender, and language(s) your audience know.

As you will make these selections, your audience size indicator on the right side the screen will shift. It will show the result in the form of potential reach with your selection of audience.

Detailed Targeting: Detailed targeting reach a very specific audience. Using a detailed targeting feature, you can go very specific in Facebook advertising. You can target or exclude people by providing all the information such as demographics, behaviors or interests.

Connections: This feature either target your existing audience or new audience. Include people who are your existing connections on your Facebook page, apps and events by selecting people or friends of people who like your page, people or friends of people who used your app or people who responded to your event respectively. However, if you want to reach a new audience, then you have to select exclude people options.

Step # 5 – Facebook Ad Placements

This portion of the ad set provides simple choices

of placements such as automatic placements or edit placements.

If you select automatic placements, Facebook will target your audience by placing your advertisement across platforms such as Facebook, Instagram, Audience Network and Messenger.

An alternate is choosing your ad placements options by selecting "Edit Placements." You will see already checked places for ad placements, while unchecked places are unavailable for ads.

Scroll down more to select specific mobile devices or operating systems. The available options are android phones, iOS phone, and feature phones.

You can also exclude certain categories to prevent your ads from appearing in sensitive places such as debatable social issues, tragedy and conflict, content that is mature or relates to dating, and gambling.

Step # 6 – Budget and Scheduling

In this portion of the ad set, you decide how much budget should be allocated to your Facebook advertising.

Budget: Write the amount you would like to spend on your paid Facebook ads in the space of "Budget."

Schedule: There are two options. Either you can run ad immediately or schedule to start on a certain date.

The most efficient way to spend your social media advertising budget is to run on a schedule.

Click on "Show Advanced Options" to optimize your ad budget.

When you have made selections for your audience, ad placements, their budget and scheduling, and you are happy with the audience number indicated on audience size indicator, click "Continue."

Step # 7 – Create Advert

First either select "create an ad" to produce your ad from scratch, or you can use your ever-green post for your ad in "Use Existing Post" option.

Identity: The identity box of your ad will show your Facebook business name page. You need this Facebook page to connect to its Instagram page. If you don't have one, set up a business Instagram account.

Format: Format box provides features to add a look to your ad. Browse through the available templates and select the one which makes your ad eye-catching.

Check instant experience box to introduce your products or services to new customers. This is optional.

Media: The media box provide you add multiple images or videos to your ad. See the right side of your screen to make sure your media meet the recommended size and file type for the Facebook ad.

Recommended image specifications are:

Size: 1080 by 1080 pixels

Crop: 1:1

File format: .jpg or .png

Recommended video specifications are

Resolution: minimum 600 Pixels width

Ratio: 4:5

File size: up to 4 GB

File format:.mp4, .mov, .gif

Link: Link box is where you write a copy for your ad. Write benefits or offers of your products or services in the text box. Use power words and write the copy in a clear and concise manner. Read "Copywriting for Social Media Ads" in chapter 2 for effective copywriting. Track conversion and ad performance by setting up Facebook Pixel, any app event, or offline events.

When you are happy with your ad, show it to your friends and family and gather their feedback. Maybe you will get a better idea about how to improve your ad.

Click on "confirm" to submit your ad. Once Facebook approves your ad, you will get a notification in your email account.

Types of Facebook Ads:

It's important to understand the different types of Facebook ads and their text and object specifics.

1- Facebook Photo Ads

Photo ad is a simple ad and a great way to get started with Facebook advertising. You can create one with just a few clicks, either by uploading a new image or boosting an existing photo post from your Facebook wall.

Campaign objectives: All objectives, except

for getting video views

Headline: 30 characters

Description: 125 characters

Link description: 25 characters

2- **Facebook Video Ads**

Advertising through video is not new on Facebook, but recently it has proven the most effective advertising tool. Through a video ad, you can show your product in action, a service improving your user life, or it can be just inspirational.

Campaign objectives: All objectives, except for getting video views

Headline: 30 characters

Description: 125 characters

Link description: 30 characters

3- **Facebook Carousel Ads**

Carousel ads scroll multiple images or videos, maximum 10, to showcase one or different products or services. Moreover, you can see this ad space to highlight multiple benefits your product can provide to your audience.

Campaign objectives: All objectives, except for engagement and getting video views

Headline: 40 characters

Description: 125 characters

Link description: 20 characters

4- **Facebook Slideshow Ads**

A Facebook Slideshow ad is a simple and easy way to create short product videos from existing videos or photos. If you don't have your own video or image, you can use stock photos to create this ad. You can add text and music as well. The slideshow ads have eye-catching motion, but they use much less bandwidth and hence load easily even on slow internet connections.

Campaign objectives: All objectives, except for getting video views

Headline: 25 characters

Description: 125 characters

Link description: 30 characters

5- Facebook Collection Ads

A collection advert is for mobile devices only. It allows showcasing one or multiple products that your customer could be interested in buying. They make online shopping very easy for the people that are on the go or have a slow internet connection. Plus, when paired with instant experiences, your customer won't leave

Facebook without purchasing your product.

Campaign objectives: Only for conversions, traffic, catalog sales, and store visits

Headline: 25 characters

Description: 90 characters

Link description: Not applicable

6- **Facebook Instant Experience Ads**

Formerly called as Canvas ads, Instant experience ads are full-screen ads that bring products and brands to life. They load instantly, now fifteen times faster than standard Facebook and mobile websites.

Campaign objectives: All objectives, except for lead generation, messages and catalog sales

Headline: No limits, use Facebook's templates

Description: No limits, use Facebook's templates

Link description: No limits, use Facebook's templates

7- **Facebook Lead Ads**

Just like the name suggests, lead ads are a great way to feed your Facebook sales funnel. They are specifically designed for mobile devices so that your target audience can easily share their contact information without tying a lot. You can use these ads for newsletter subscriptions or signing up some users for your product trial. They usually have a call-to-action button, such as sign up.

Campaign objectives: For lead generation

Headline: 25 characters

Description: 125 characters

Link description: 30 characters

8- Facebook Dynamic Ads

Through dynamic ads, you can reach to those customers that are most interested in purchasing your product or service. For example, that potential customer could be someone who has visited your product page or have placed it in their shopping cart on your website but haven't checked out; a dynamic advert will appear in that customer Facebook feed to remind them to complete their actions and make the purchase.

Campaign objectives: For conversions, catalog sales and store visits

Headline: 25 characters

Description: 125 characters

Link description: Not applicable

9- **Facebook Messenger Ads**

You can send all of the above mentioned Facebook ads through Facebook messenger. So, when you are creating your ad, simply choose messenger along with your Facebook feed. You can also use "click-to-messenger" advertisements that allows a call-to-action button that open messenger conversation with customer service.

Campaign objectives: All objective, except for engagements, video views, lead generation, and store visits

Headline: 25 characters

Description: 125 characters

Link description: Not applicable

Monitoring Facebook Advert

Campaign

Now that your Facebook ad campaign is up and running, you need to monitor it so that you can make any necessary changes against the incoming data such as editing, stopping ads, increasing ad budget, etc.. Here are some tips to keep track of your ad campaign statistics on Facebook.

1- Make Facebook ads manager your homepage. Obviously, Facebook ads manager will be your most regularly visited page during the ad campaign. Click on the ad, and you will get to see all the reports and statistics for this particular ad. Facebook ad manager provides a summary for your ad campaign, shows you how well they are running, your daily spending, a report of total impressions, and how many clicks you have received. Check demographic information to see how much money you have spent and if your ad is actually being view or not. If you are not happy with the results of your ad, stop it and make adjustments such as changing the target audience, modifying the headline, updating the copy, and changing images.

2- Analyze the data properly. Ad manager provides you data using specific terms so you must understand them fully to analyze data and make necessary changes in the campaign. For example, measure your reach to the target audience with indicators on ad manager. On Facebook ad manager, targeted audience denotes to prospect viewers set by you when you were creating an ad campaign. Similarly, the reach of your ad means number of Facebook users that has seen your ad, frequency means the number of times a single user has seen your ad, and social reach means the number of friends of people that have seen your ad. Similarly, you can measure the performance of your ad by making a comparison between the actions and clicks on your ad.

3- Use Facebook reports. Click on the report tab in your ad manager and analyze various reports by choosing parameters such as report type, time range, and format, etc.. You will get an advertising performance report, responder demographics report, actions by impression time report, and inline interaction report. Use the first report all the time to manage your ad's performance. These reports provide an in-depth understanding and performance of your advertisement and explain how to optimize it. Furthermore, these reports will give you better information about your target audience engagement with your ad, and in this way, you will find out how successful your targeting is.

4- Compare current ad performance with the previous one. Take time to look at the statistics in your current report and compare with the previous results. Are your statics improving or declining? What was different in your ad campaign this time? What worked well in this ad campaign compared to the previous one? Create a log of these type of question as this data will provide you with possibilities to create better ad campaigns.

Even if you are running a Facebook ad campaign for the first time, download your performance reports and keep them safe to compare with your future campaigns. These reports will serve as a reference to inform you what worked before and what didn't work so that you can keep these points in them while creating and running your new ad campaigns.

Best Practices for Facebook Ads in 2019

Facebook is constantly changing. So what are the best practices through which you can ensure your ad achieve the performance it deserves in 2019?

Practice # 1 – Use Visual Power

Working with visuals always requires hard work, and it gets harder to do advertising on Facebook. On Facebook, people easily scroll down ads or just ignore them; your ad can capture its audience attention in an instant with top-notch visuals. So if you have locked your ad with the power of visual the most, then your ad is a winner.

Practice # 2 – Relevance Is Key

One important thing you always have to remember while creating your ad is to make it fully enticing for the target audience and the market. Creating a highly relevant advert will save not only time but also your investment and it will deliver exactly what your audience wants. So, if your ad succeeds in keeping your audience happy and interested, then they will keep on enjoying your advertisements in the future as well. For this, you have to understand the psychology of your audience well to ensure your

Facebook target audience and ad copy is up to the mark.

Practice # 3 - Effective Value Proposition

Value proposition means how a business describe their users and why they should use their service or buy their product. You have to prove to your users that your product is what they have looking for and is their best option. To achieve this, deliver your product value in the ad copy in an alluring, clear and concise manner. If your ad delivers an effective value proposition of product, your user will be more likely to click on your ad.

Practice # 4 – Call-To-Action or Nothing

Though Facebook sale funnel starts with educating people about your brand and conducting engagements, all the efforts will go down the drain if you get fail to entice the customer to click on your call-to-action. So be sure to always leave a sense of urgency in your ad that will make your potential customer click on your ad and make the purchase. The best way to ensure that your user sees the CTA on your ad is to use a clear call-to-action sign with clear instructions in the ad copy.

Practice # 5 – Be Frugal with the Budget in Your First Ad Campaign

If your brand is new, then you need to grab the attention of your prospect customers by using a multi-ad structure. This can be easily done by setting up multiple ads within a single ad set in your Facebook ad manager. Start with the budget of about $150 to $ 300 or more for the set, run the ad and monitor performance before you expand the ad campaign. If your ad is not meeting your marketing goal, then stop running it, take out its budget and put it into an ad that can work.

Practice # 6 – Measure Results and Make Adjustments in Your Ad

Of course, your ad campaigns will take time to evolve, learn, grow, and perform better. So it is important for you to keep learning from the response and actual sales of your Facebook ad campaign. Don't just focus on the number of likes or shares. Instead, analyze results to determine how much traffic your ad target, how much sales your advert bring in and then use this valuable information to make adjustments in your future ads accordingly.

Chapter 4: Advertising with Instagram

For growing businesses and building brands, it is important to utilize all the power of advertising channels, and for this, social media platforms are becoming a go-to. It's no doubt that Facebook holds first rank and first preference of every marketer for advertising, but there is another fast-growing social media platform that offers an extensive range of marketing tools, Instagram. Instagram is open to all companies, whether large or small, to get their message in front of a more diverse audience.

With more than 1,000 million monthly users, Instagram proved itself a massive platform for building brands and connecting audience in 2018 and it will keep catering advertisers with its highly effective ads in 2019 as well. That's why Instagram advertising should be part of your social media marketing strategy for 2019.

When Facebook purchased a photo-sharing app "Instagram" in 2012, no one foresaw its 30 million user's community booming into more 1 billion users in the next seven years. That's a lot of progress, and this has led to a lot of improvement in the advertising area of Instagram, all thanks to the power of its parent company, Facebook.

Only social media platform such as Facebook and YouTube have more logging in, but did you know 500 million of them are using Instagram daily?

Moreover, 80 percent of Instagram users are outside the U.S. This large percent holds a lot of potential to generate advertisement revenue for your products and services. With estimates of more than 7 billion in mobile advertising revenue in 2019. So, if you are interested in doing business in Turkey, Japan, or Dubai, then Instagram is the place to make great sales for your global products. People under 25 years use Instagram 32 minutes a day, compared to 24 minutes per day for 25 years old and older. And this is more than before.

Over 200 million users visit at least one business profile every day. Whether it is clothing or lingerie, you will find 97 percent of fashion brands on Instagram. With such a high count of users and rich engagement level, Instagram is the platform where real business goals can be achieved. This is a great opportunity for brands to connect with the audience, whether on the go or in the moment. In fact, in 2019 Instagram will become home to new brands.

But who are these 1 billion Instagram users?

As an advertiser, understanding Instagram demographics is critical so that you know well about the people who are the part of its audience and who is actually going to see your advert.

Well, Instagram is ruled by millennials. Here is a detailed breakdown of its demographic.

Age 13 to 17: 7% - 70 million users

Age 18 to 24: 32% - 320 million users

Age 25 to 34: 32% - 320 million users

Age 35 to 44: 15% - 150 million users

Age 45 to 54: 8% - 80 million users

Age 55 to 64: 3% - 30 million users

Age 65+: 2% - 20 million users

So, are you one of these Instagram users? Is your business also connecting with this large audience?

If you have been spending your ad budget on video advertising through Facebook, then in 2019 you should absolutely run a dual campaign on Instagram to test and compare your results. By running your Facebook video ad, together with an Instagram video ad, you will get your double reach to the audience, double exposure, and access to billions of more users.

Features and Benefits of Advertising on Instagram

Below are features and benefits that Instagram advertising offers over other social media marketing channels.

- Instagram and Facebook are connected and this makes targeting your audience easier with just using Facebook data and advertising tools. All advertising schedules, budgeting, and setting up ad campaigns are done through the Facebook Ad manager. So you need to start from scratch or learn the operation of another advertising tool for Instagram, once you have used Facebook for marketing and advertising.

- Instagram offers a customizable CTA button. Call of Action buttons ensure that your advertising creates the highest probability of its desired response, such as a purchase or whether an ad can motivate someone to convert into a lead or, much better, into a regular paying customer. Instagram offers five unique call-to-actions to advertisers, allowing them to create a better ad that fits to target a specific audience. With these CTA buttons, you can do anything, whether linking your website to download an application or an online store to shop for your products.

- Instagram has a boundless audience. With over 1 billion users following and growing, along with broad networking capabilities, Instagram has turned out an essential tool for an increase in sales and growth of the business through effectively constructed marketing efforts. Instagram can introduce your brand to its mega-sized audience and target a specific audience based on demographics, user behaviors, company goals, intent, and even using their locations.

- Another benefit that advertiser can get from Instagram is its performance tracking capabilities. Being part of Facebook, advertisers can use a Facebook ad manager to check whether their highly targeted ads are performing like they should or not. Advertisers can track the most important metrics and even optimize ad content to yield the best results. In addition, advertisers can customize ads based on the range of targeting factors. You can even conduct A/B testing of your ad in just clicks.

- Instagram ads are non-intrusive, therefore, these ads are less likely to annoy your audience. As a result, Instagram ads return with the best results in terms of cost and returns on investment (ROI). Also, Instagram advertising in more effective and less time consuming.

A/B Testing

A/B testing is a marketing strategy that dates back to the days when there was no internet, when direct mail was used to conduct a small test on a contact list for estimating the cost of printing and mailing a campaign.

Back at those times, A/B testing was quite time-consuming. Fortunately, for today's marketers, A/B testing can be conducted in real time, thus allowing marketers to refine their marketing and advertising strategies on the fly.

To perform A/B testing, you need to split your audience into two groups, showing each group with a different marketing strategy and then comparing the responses to determine which marketing strategy is the most effective one.

It is important to understand that only one variation should be used at a time. So, if you want to test multiple headlines, different images, or different style of ads, you will need to conduct multiple A/B tests.

So, what social media marketing components can A/B test?

Text:

The type and style of language in your core message or copy in your social media advert definitely need extensive testing. For example, you could test

- Number of character in post
- Post style, like a question against statement or quote against key statistics
- Use of emoji in text
- Numbered lists or digits in post
- Punctuation
- The tone of message like casual against formal, active against passive, and so on.

Headline and Description:

The headline is highly visible in the ad and is important to enhance. You can apply the A/B tests for text to test different headlines and descriptions.

Call-To-Action:

CTA is incredibly important in advertising because it's where you ask your audience to engage. Getting your CTA right is critical, so be sure to A/B test its various approaches.

Image or Video:

As mentioned before, ads with image or video perform best and therefore, it is important to test videos and images with your audience and on each social media platform. You could test:

- Text only ads with ads containing an image or video
- Animated gifs against regular image or other image types
- Photo of products against Infographics
- Length of video

Ad Format:

Test different formats of the ad to see which one is most effective for your content. For example, carousel ads may work best for announcing your new products through Facebook advertising, but

Instagram story ads work best to make potential customers aware of your store.

Hashtags:

Hashtags extend the reach of Instagram marketing post. So, you need to find out if they are annoying your audience or driving more engagement and this can be with social media A/B testing. You could also test:

- Single hashtag against multiple hashtags
- One hashtag with other
- Brand hashtags versus another industry hashtag
- Which hashtags gives the best engagement result in a particular industry?
- Hashtag placement in the copy of your ad, whether at the start, in the middle or at the end.

Target Audience:

A/B testing of the target audience is a little different because it tells how a particular audience responds to an ad. This is done by showing the same ad to a different audience to see which audience segment gives a better response. Your targeting option for A/B testing can be base on gender, language, social media platform, devices or specific user characteristics like their purchase behavior or interests.

The results can help you create a specialized advertising strategy and campaign for each audience segments.

Now, coming to run an A/B test on social media, it can be done by following this basic structure.

1- Choose any of the above-mentioned elements to test.
2- Research for existing ideas of the particular element to know what will work best.
3- Use your research knowledge to create two variations, remembering that only one element differs between the variations.
4- Expose each segment of your audience with each variation.

5- Monitor the responses and analyze your results.

6- Choose the winning variation. You can test this variation against another small variations to see if your results improve further.

Start the process over again.

Types of Instagram Ads

Instagram offers five types of ads.

1- Photo Ads

Instagram photo or image ads allow businesses to share their story or showcase their product through eye-captivating images. So if you have top-notch visual content of your brand, then Instagram image ads give you the platform to share it with your target specific audience.

Ad format: a photo image appear in landscape, vertical or square format.

Always remembers these three objectives for Instagram photo ads.

- Incorporate a brand logo in images. In this way, you make sure that your images are on brand. Find different and unique ways to incorporate your brand icon, logo, or even color scheme in recognizable size so that your target audience who is trying to reach them.

- Your images should deliver your business message. Your image should make people think or feel something different when they see your ad. Ask yourself these questions: what do you want your message to be? How do you want your audience to describe your brand or product? The answers to these questions will help in selecting the best image for your ad and will explain how to tailor your Instagram ad.

- Your image should be well crafted. This doesn't mean that your Instagram ad image should be beautiful. When you are capturing an image for Instagram business, keep a strong focal point that can be your brand icon, logo or anything recognizable to your target audience, and make sure lighting and framing of the image are appropriate. A clear and straightforward photo is likely to present your brand or business more appropriate through the Instagram ad.

2- **Video Ads**

Instagram is a perfect platform to capitalize on video format to capture the target audience's attention. In fact, time spent watching videos on Instagram is more than 80 percent year after year and growing. Instagram video advertising is divided into two categories; In-stream video ads and story ads.

- In-stream video ads are identical to in-stream Instagram posts, with the exception that these posts have a CTA button that drives the intended audience to a certain action such as learn more or other similar call-to-actions. The following ad is the example of the in-stream video ad.

Ad format: Landscape, vertical or square format.

Landscape Ad resolution: 66 by 315 or 1:9 aspect ratio

Vertical Ad resolution: 600 by 750 or 4:5 aspect ratio

Square Ad resolution: 60 by 600 or 1:1 aspect ratio

Ad length: maximum of 60 seconds

File size: maximum of 4 GB

Frame per second: 30 FPS

Ad type: .mp4, .mov

Caption length: maximum of 125 characters

3- Story Ads

Though story ads are part of Instagram video ads, now they are treated as an individual ad category. A sponsored label appears in the top-right corner of the story and reveals that your story is an ad, not part of your daily Instagram stories. More than 300 million Instagram users view stories day; there is a huge audience that you can reach through your story ad. Story ads or full-screen ads show up in the stories section of Instagram like a commercial break, where user view disappearing video content that lasts for only 24 hours. Therefore, stories ads are perfect opportunities to share limited time offers or promotions of your product to the target audience. The call-to-action is in the form of a swipe button that directly takes the audience to website from the ad. Furthermore, Instagram stories features like face filters, video effects, and text for captions that make it a fun and creative activity. Here are specifications for story video ads

Video resolution: minimum 600 by 1067 and maximum 1080 by 1920 Pixels

Aspect ratio: 9:16

Ad length: maximum of 15 seconds

File size: maximum 4 GB

Ad type: .mp4, .mov

4- **Carousels Ads**

Being a part of the Facebook family, Instagram has adopted its carousal-style advertising for video and photo ads. Using this ad, businesses can show a series of images or videos of their products or brands in a slide show presentation with a call-to-action underneath it that directly takes the potential customer to your website. Carousels ads offer versatility and the creative space to tell longer stories of your business or brand by highlighting multiple products or benefits of one product in up to 2 to 10 photos or videos. These Instagram ads are perfect for brands that have diverse assets like fashion or food.

5- **Canvas Ads**

Just like a Facebook Canvas ad, Instagram advertisers can use an array of Facebook Canvas template to create immersive video content for Instagram stories. This ad can be optimized for mobile and load quickly. Hence canvas ads provide a smooth viewing experience and are perfect for low internet connection.

Best Practices for Instagram Video Ads in 2019

- **Follow Facebook**

Video content that performs well on Facebook is more likely to perform well on Instagram too. So start your advertising campaign by running those Facebook ads on Instagram that gave the best performance and see how it goes.

- **Keep Videos Short and Sweet**

Keep your Instagram video ads short and snappy. Story ads are a maximum of 15 seconds long, and you have to get the attention of your target audience in the first 3 seconds. If you succeed in grabbing attention in the first few seconds, then your audience is hooked to your ad.

- **Caption Key Phrases**

If your Instagram ad is sound-off, then draw your viewer's attention with a handful of captions. But don't try to caption everything. Less is more!

- **Call-To-Action**

Try embedding your call-to-action in the middle of the video ad. Statistics show that the viewer's conversions are highest when CTA's are right in the middle of the ad, compared to opening or ending.

- **Think like a Gif**

Of course, you would want your ad to watch multiple times. So, make your Instagram ad watchable by designing it to play as a perfect loop. If viewers found it interesting enough, they will likely let the ad play a few more times.

- **Make Vertical Stories**

  The best way to let Instagram story ads provide an immersive experience to your viewers is to film them in vertical format, in full-screen.

- **Don't Run Ad Marathons**

  One Instagram ad is not enough to achieve your marketing goal, so create multiple Instagram video ads. Focus each video ad on one problem in your viewer's life and offer a solution or your product benefit that makes your viewer's life easier.

Tips to Turn Stories Ads into Sales

Keep Your Story Message Short and Straight

Your key ad message for Instagram story ads should be short, sweet, and to the point. Your story ads are not part of your day-to-day Instagram stories, and this means that once your audience realizes that your story is an ad, they can be more likely to swipe away from your story. And you don't want that. So to create a story ad that converts, it's important to present a punchy core message quickly that is easy to read. Moreover, the video content is simple, and that means no essays.

Don't Forget Your Brand Logo

Adding your brand icon to Instagram ads seems like a basic tip, but it is essential if you aim to reach more audiences and improve brand awareness. Your Instagram story ads are viewed by the target audience on the basis of demographics you select for your campaign, which means your audience may not have heard about your business or product before. So, if you are reaching an audience who is unaware of you, including your icon or brand in the ad is key. If you don't have a logo, then place your brand or product name in the top-right corner of the ad.

Kind Your Brand in Mind in Your Stories Ads

Make sure that your Instagram story ads fit seamlessly with your overall brand aesthetic. Your Instagram story ad aims to keep your users engaged and increase brand recognition, even if it is just for a few seconds. Think about typography and imagery of your ad; they always reflect your brand aesthetics. The easiest way to do this is by using colorful images, typeface, and color schemes that perfectly align with your brand and show off your products in a lighthearted and fun way.

Polished Instagram Stories Aren't the Best Choice for Ads

You have to pour your blood, sweat, and budget into your story ads to make them successfully meet your advertising objectives. People watch Instagram stories causally, so if they come across a commercial video, their immediate reaction could be to swipe away.

In fact, Instagram stories ads should reflect authenticity and be real.

You might have spotted an influencer talking about a brand or product by just talking into the camera. This type of ad is more informal and drives fewer sales, resulting in an ad that is more personal and keeps an audience engaged.

Create a Strong Call-To-Action

Nothing beats a strong call-to-action like a limited deal or exclusive offer. Creating urgency within your Instagram story ads is one simple way to engage users with the ad, to encourage viewers to swipe on the CTA, visit your website, and there hopefully make a purchase. Use a strong call-to-action in your ad in the text which urges your user to swipe up to learn more by visiting your website.

Position Text Strategically in Story Ads

Instagram users are wary of Instagram story ads and sponsored ads. So, if you don't want your audience to draw away from sponsored tagged ads, place your core message and graphics in the middle or close to your swipe-up link. Remember, every second of your ad counts when it comes to engagement. So, if you get successful in catching your target viewer's eye immediately with your messages and graphics, not the sponsored tag, then your Instagram stories could make a huge difference.

Use Carousel Ads for Longer Messages

If you think your advertising message is not fit for one 15 second video story, that's exactly why you should use Instagram carousel ads for Instagram story ads. Carousel ads, which can be made with a maximum of three images or three 15-second videos, enable you to build your message through three parts. Users can tap through, swipe back and forth, or pause the video content whenever they like. So it is important to pay more attention to creativity and engaging from the get-go. If your first part of the ad is fun, then your users will be more likely to tap through the next part to learn more.

Add Music to Your Instagram Story Ads

Instagram story ads get more engagement with the sound on. Having a background score, whether any music or voice over, can make your ad more engaging and draw more audiences in. So try it out next time in your story ads.

Before you start to create your ad, decide what goal your Instagram is trying to achieve.

Goals for Instagram Advertisements

Following are four main goals for your Instagram video campaigns and types of videos that are best for them.

Goal # 1 – Attract a New Audience

You can optimize your Instagram campaign for brand awareness and for this, attract as many users as possible and aware them with your brand or product.

- **Use in-stream commercials up to 15 seconds long to promote your brand or product or use time-lapse video to capture new audience attention.**
- **Use story ads with a carousal feature or creative educational video and tell a mini-story to highlight your brand impact on your customer lives or in your industry.**

Goal # 2 – Engage More Visitors

If your Instagram ad campaign is to engage with more views, then you must get the right type of audience to take action. Therefore, optimize your campaign to drive traffic to your page or video views to make sure the right audience is watching it.

- Try testimonials, tutorials, or product video in in-stream ads to inspire your audience to learn more about your business.
- For story ads, give your users a sneak peek in the life video that looks like the content your audience is creating. Make the story

ad compelling enough, and they will be motivated to take action.

Goal # 3 – Nurture Leads to Regular Customers

If you are generating enough leads, then it is time to optimize Instagram advertising campaigns for conversions which also helps to lower cost per action. Promote specific sales or services or products directly through the video.

- Try doing FAQ video through the in-stream ad, answering the questions your leads might have in their buyer's stage. You can also share a 60-second product review video; this transparently represents your service or product.
- Create customer spotlight videos for story ads that highlight your customer success stories. Or try creating a video of a recent event.

Setting up an Instagram Business profile

Here is everything you need to know about using Instagram for business, whether running Instagram ads or to add links to Instagram stories.

Step # 1 – Create a Facebook Page for Your Business

Your business must have a Facebook presence. If you already have a Facebook business page, skip to the next step.

And if not, then head over to chapter 3 "Advertising with Facebook" and learn to create a business page under the head "how to advertise on Facebook."

Step # 2 – Connect Your Facebook Business Page to the Instagram Account

If you have a personal Instagram account with appropriate brand content, then you might convert it to a business page.

1- Log in to your Instagram account (personal one) on the app and go to your profile.

2- Next, tap the three lines icon at the top-right corner of the app and then tap "settings."

3- There, in the options tap "switch to business profile" option and then tap continue.

4- Connect your profile to the Facebook business page by adding details such as business category and contact information.

5- Tap "done."

If you don't have an Instagram account, then you can set up an Instagram account from scratch with these steps.

1- Download the Instagram app.

2- Tap the Instagram app to open it and sign up with the admin account ID and relevant username and password. You can also log in with Facebook.

3- Tap next, fill in your profile information and then tap done.

4- Now you can convert your account into a business account by following the above steps.

That's it. Now that you have an Instagram business profile connected to the Facebook page associated with your business, you can now focus on creating a winning Instagram advertising campaign.

How to Advertise on Instagram

Advertisers recognize the potential of Instagram for business. And to robust its advertising experience, Instagram continues to add incredible features and functionality that has made advertising on Instagram extremely easy and efficient. Backed by the power of Facebook, advertisers can now use a Facebook ad manager to create an Instagram ad campaign and manage and analyze them.

Step # 1 – Do Some Research

But before heading to Facebook Ad manager, you need to spend some time researching on your competitors Instagram accounts. Ask yourself these questions:

What types of ads are your competitor running?

What CTA do they use?

How much engagement their posts and ads are getting?

Next, go to their product page, scroll it to notice details, copy and graphics of their images and click on specific products.

Also, go their bio and visit their mobile site by clicking on its link in their bio. When you are done exploring their website, go back to Instagram account and scroll your feed. There is a very good chance that you will see the Instagram ad from that competitor's page.

Repeat this process with different competitors to get a sense of what types of ads are running on Instagram.

Step # 2 – Creating an Instagram Advertising Campaign

Creating an Instagram advertising campaign is the same as Facebook advertising. They have the same campaign objectives, targeting, custom audience feature, and advertising creative.

1- First, you have to connect Instagram account with a Facebook business account, as mentioned in the previous heading.

2- Then go to Facebook Ads manager to create an advertising campaign. To create your ad set, go to chapter 3 and the steps mentioned in "how to advertise on Facebook" will walk you through the advertising steps.

By following these steps, you will pick your campaign objectives. For video ads, it is best to select video views under the consideration block.

Then create your Ad set by defining your audience, budget, scheduling and ad placements. Once you are done with Ad set configuration, click continue and develop it in ad creative. Upload visuals, add text, headline, and call-to-actions. If your campaign objective is traffic or conversions, you will be able to use customize call-to-action buttons in your link button.

Preview the ad and if you are pleased with your ad, run it on Facebook and Instagram. If you want to run an ad on Instagram only, make sure other ad distribution options have been unchecked.

Step # 3 – Track Your Ad Conversions and Engagement

Keep a close eye on the performance metrics of your Instagram ad. If you want your campaign to produce the best results, you need to analyze these metrics and edit and optimize your campaign accordingly. Performance metrics and reports are available in the Facebook Ads manager, and you will be able to look at campaign and ad set metrics and ad levels. You will also be able to see performance reports, save them and customize columns in the Facebook Ads Manager.

Remember, metrics don't always tell the complete story. You have to look beyond the numbers and pay attention to indicators of engagement. These include comments in your ads, keeping track of niche or segment in your industry, especially influential followers.

Read more information about monitoring your advertising campaign under the heading "Monitoring Facebook Advert Campaign" in chapter 3.

To Sum up...

It is essential to do some research before you start your Instagram ad campaign. You must choose the right campaign objective because it plays a vital role in optimizing your ad, how you pay and track them.

If your advertising campaign objective is increasing conversions or remarketing ads to users who visit your website, then you need to install Facebook Pixel on your website first. Read more about Facebook Pixel and how it gathers user data in chapter 3.

When you are developing your Instagram ad, you should think about your marketing objective object, the audience you are targeting and the message that will motivate users to engage with your ad.

Once your ad campaign is up and running, you need to monitor its performance to edit and optimize it constantly.

And, always start with a small budget. If your Instagram advertisement performs better in a low budget, then you can increase the budget every three days. And if doesn't, shut off your campaign and create a new one.

Best practices for Instagram Ads in 2019

Here are some best tips to keep in mind that will help you create great ads for Instagram.

3- Know Your Audience:

Never forget who you are trying to reach. Your right target customer is more than a set of demographics or interests. If you want your ad to return the best results, then you have to learn how to reach the right people. Pay attention to what your audience need or want and what product or service you are offering to them. Keep their values and goals in mind as you create an ad campaign. And, once you have their attention, make the most of it and convert them.

4- Leverage User-Generated Content:

If your ad is receiving good viewing rates, then you know what your user love, likes and follows. But this not enough to build real connections and engagements with users. To strengthen your bond with users, share user-generated content. It can third-party endorsement or social proof of your business's value. By sharing this content, you are not only building strong relationships online, but you are also extra value to your products with minimal expenditure in money and time.

5- Use Text Wisely:

Instagram ads are more about visuals so you can't use much text in the Instagram ads. So use words wisely, about 22000 characters, to add a nice caption to your ad and while writing something about your ad, keep your audience persona in mind. Your effective writing will make your audience click on your drive and drive traffic to the website for purchase or download an app.

6- Create an Experience:

Each element of your Instagram advert should represent who you are as a company or brand. The visuals, message, tone, everything is important. So present your brand in the best manner through your Instagram ads.

7- Highlight Your Customer:

It is a great way to showcase your customers for building authentic connections online while you promote your brand. If you want your product to be the most stimulating on visually driven platforms, then your customers may able to add extra value to your brand. Capture and deliver customer stories in a relatable style. This strategy will drastically boost your engagement through the advert.

8- Keep It Fresh:

Catching attention with a killer ad is easy. Obviously, you don't want your audience to tune out from your ad, so switch ads regularly like every well or two, to keep them interested in your products. Another benefit of changing the ad is that you will learn which of the ads work best. Experiment ads with different formats, captions, and audiences.

9- Use the Right Hashtags:

Instagram provides more engagement compared to other social media advertising platforms. The secret is

Instagram hashtags that not only boost engagement, but they also increase brand awareness. You can use up to 30 hashtags each time but don't think of quantity, instead focus on quality. Add hashtags that are relevant to your audience and popular in your industry. You are master the art of hashtag with these simple guidelines:

- Compete with your ad using your competitor's hashtags. Maybe you will new hashtags to add to your ad, or you can always search for alternative hashtags.

- Learn from the best. Add hashtags that are used by influential people in your industry or someone who has a well-established audience.

- Search hashtags from the Instagram search function. Type a relevant keyword on the Instagram search bar, select the tag tab, and you will get hashtags with that keyword along with a number of post with it. Use a combination of some short and easy, popular and niche hashtags to find your product a sweet spot.

Chapter 5: Advertising with YouTube

As mentioned before, the video is a powerful tactic to advertise. Its limitless power is perfect to reach masses, create awareness for brands and considerations. People aren't just looking for passive viewing experience through engaging videos; they also crave for something more interactive. Furthermore, video marketing is an evolving marketing strategy due to its more action-oriented approach in recent years.

Historically, video marketing hasn't been optimizable or actionable, and neither measurable against direct response objectives for business. But that changed when YouTube came in the limelight. With time, it has gone through many evolutions of advertising options such as debuting its participatory ads and brand channels in 2006. These ads offer a new doorway for businesses to reach a wider audience with their video content. Over the years, more advertisement options and advertisement campaign tools have been developed that have made advertising on YouTube more appealing than ever before.

With 2 billion YouTube users logging in, over 1 billion hours of video content viewed daily, 5 billion daily video views and over 3 billion searches per month, YouTube has been declared the second most popular search engine and favorite video sharing platform in 2018 and YouTube will maintain this position in 2019 too.

The number don't lie. Each video has an opportunity to expose an ad to someone who could be interested in what that business offer.

Ninety-nine percent business who use YouTube for video advertising in says they will continue to do so in 2019. Such a high growth of advertisers and viewers on YouTube means more competition. Also, organic reach to the audience and getting more views to your ads is not enough. The solution - YouTube paid advertising campaigns which have made the reach to the right audience both easier and customizable than ever before.

It is estimated that 80 percent of all internet traffic will be video content by 2021. So if you have a business, but you are advertising it on YouTube yet, now is the perfect time to start reaping its benefits for your business.

Here comes a more bugging question – why use YouTube for video marketing Instead of Facebook, Twitter or Instagram Ads.

YouTube is the oldest social media platform in the game of video marketing. Being around since 2005 and having the support of parent company Google, YouTube is crushing the game and giving tough competition to other social media platforms for advertising.

Another important reason that gives YouTube an edge in video marketing is its trade approach what comes from their users. YouTube users are already prime viewers when they come to this platform to watch video ads, whether searching for specific topics or visiting the homepage. Hence, YouTube allows businesses to target the intended audience, and they only have to pay when their audience see their ad.

Moreover, unlike other social media platforms, YouTube users don't have to log in to watch video advert. Yes, this makes targeting options less accurate on YouTube, but as YouTube ads are set up through Google Ads, this means your business can get access to google information when targeting potential customer. Also, add in the option to directly target potential customers with video advertisements based on their previous searches.

Coming to the best part about video advertising is that keywords on YouTube are less costly than on Google. Google keywords cost between $1 to $2, while advertising on YouTube is under $0.1 per click.

Best YouTube Advertising Practices

While the best practice to get most from your video advertising on YouTube relates to your goal, but here some more practices that you should into consideration before you plan your own YouTube video advertising campaign.

- **Keep the Ad Under 0:45**

  According to Google, one of the reasons viewers lose interest in the end if it is too long. Most of the viewer's drop significantly after 45 seconds of running time of an ad. If you don't want your ad to be one of these ignored ads, then make a point to keep the running time under 45 seconds.

- **Give Your Ads a Relevant Title**

  Your ad title will first capture your viewer attention. So if you want your ad to deliver the right first impression, then keep your title simple, to the point and should match your user's search terms. If your YouTube ad title is irrelevant, the user won't click on it.

- **Nail the Thumbnail**

Your ad thumbnail should be appealing that will make your ad stand out. Select that thumbnail which represents your video and brand. You can either create your own or use a still from your video, but of course in high-quality.

- **Sync Your Marketing**

You have to tailor your landing page so that it relates well to the video content of your ad. If you overworked on your landing page, your audience might lose their interest.

- **Use Proper CTA**

Use call-to-action to encourage your ad viewer to perform an action after watching your video, such as subscribe, comment, share, watch another video and even record their response for the video.

- **Closely Monitor Your View Rate**

View rate will determine if your YouTube is working up to mark or not. The higher the viewer rate is, the more likely more viewers will engage with the video ad that will help you achieve your advertising goal. So keep a constant check on the view rate of your ad.

- **Make a Playlist**

YouTube playlist option is a great way to combine multiple advert videos in an auto play setting. So if you succeed in engaging a viewer with one ad of your playlist, playlists make it easier for them to watch more. To create a playlist:

Go to the video ad you want to advert and under the video, click "add to," then "+" sign and click on create a new playlist. Name the playlist, change the privacy setting to make ad public and finally, click "Create."

- **Use Cards and End Screens**

Use cards over your video, they look like little pop-ups, and end screens to provide a link to related content such as your channel homepage, other videos or purchase links.

- **Publish Regularly**

If you are committing to Youtube video advertising, then you publish regularly to elevate your brand in the competition. Remember, your video content of the ad doesn't need to be huge and with big price tags.

- **Use Targeted Ads to Find an Audience**

Your sales will increase if the right audience will consider it through your ads. This can be achieved by taking advantage of the interactive features of the Google Ads platform to build your YouTube advertising campaign. Once your ad is built in Google Ads platform and running, you can use its performance insights to remarket the same ads to a new audience within the display network.

Types of YouTube Video Ads Formats

There are five types of YouTube video ads formats:

1. **TrueView Ads**

The best way to drive engagement to your brand or business on YouTube is through TrueView ads. Businesses promoting their brands, products or services through TrueView ads have seen an increase in their engagement by up to 500 percent.

TrueView ads come with the option to be skipped after 5 seconds, so if you want your user to watch your whole ad, you need to make those first five seconds count. The plus point, you only have to pay when a viewer watches the ad for 30 seconds or till the ends. Therefore, TrueView ads are a safe bet for YouTube advertising. It looks like this:

Here are other reasons that explain why TrueView ads are one of the top ways to advertise on YouTube.

TrueView ads have a low risk. Using the standard TrueView ad, the audience opts in their interests of ad content, and you only have to pay when your viewer sees it for 30 seconds or more. That means the majority of the YouTube advertising budget for TrueView ads is dedicated to those specific targets who are more likely to convert.

TrueView ads are versatile. TrueView ads are best to advertise product demos, testimonials, how-to videos and more. These ads greatly affect the brands and as a result, bring in the huge source of engagement for the business.

TrueView ads have a wide reach to audiences. TrueView ads are basically a combination of the power of the YouTube search engine and Google search engine. Although TrueView ads are published on YouTube, they can be also displayed on other publisher websites in the display network depending on the ad.

TrueView ads are categorized into two types:

- **In-Stream Ads**

  Ad length: minimum of 30 seconds and a maximum of 3 minutes
  Headline: none
  Body copy: none
  Clicks on ad takes you: to your website
  Ad location: YouTube videos, Google display network, apps and games

- **Discovery Ads**

  Ad length: unlimited
  Headline: a maximum 25 characters
  Body copy: a maximum 70 characters
  Clicks on ad takes you: to your website or next video
  Ad location: YouTube videos, search results, related videos, video overlays
  You can optimize TrueView ads to reach potential customers or for action. Here's how it is done.

In 2018, Google introduced TrueView ads to reach and optimize it with respect to the advertising campaign goals. Instead of paying when the viewer sees your add, you pay on CPM basis that is the cost per 1000 views. To enable this type of optimization, an advertisement must be added between 6 and 30 seconds.

Secondly, the optimization of TrueView ads for action is done by adding a deadline and call-to-action button to your ads, such as in-stream ads. This makes your YouTube advertisements more actionable. The action can be to drive traffic to your website, generating sales or building an email list. The cost of this optimization is based on a cost per action; you pay only when the viewer clicks on the CTA button.

2. **Non-Skippable YouTube Ads**

Non-skippable advertisements are longer commercials, offering an interesting way to tell a more nuanced or deeper story. Hence, people found Non-skippable commercials annoying and often close these ads. Coming to the cost, it is based on CPM; you pay when your ad gets 1000 views.

3. **Bumper Ads**

Bumper ads are also non-Skippable adverts, but they are maligned and less irritable. Therefore, they are also on a CPM basis. The video length of the bumper ad can be a maximum of 6 seconds, and this short length makes these ads ideal for mobile, like this:

Creating a 6-second video advert sound easy but if you want your ad to meet your advertising goal, you better make its concept stronger.

4. **Overlay Ads**

Overlays ads are nothing new; you must have seen them running along the bottom of the video, whether in text form or as an image based banner. They are set up on partner videos. So if you are running a reservation sponsorship campaign, then it is best to spread the word and persuade your audience for action using overlay ads. Overlay ads appear like this during a YouTube video:

5. **In-Display Ads**

If you don't want your ad to appear within YouTube video, then you must go for display ads. A display ad appears on the right side of the user's screen and is charged on a per-view basis. In-display ads are not a prominent option as viewing this ad is by choice only if users are interested in watching the video they are currently viewing. So, if the user is really interested in your ad, they are more likely to convert. In-display ad looks like this:

6. **Sponsored Cards**

Sponsored cards are small popups, appearing as small information icon with a CTA text within the YouTube player, like this:

Sponsored cards are interactive and effective because they are unobtrusive. When the user is interested and clicks on these ads, only then they expand to their full size, like this.

YouTube Video Advertising Specifications

Before you plan to create a YouTube ad, ask yourself who is going to see it and on which device they will be watching it. Here are the different specifications and requirements for various YouTube advertisements.

Ad Type: TrueView, Non-Skippable and Bumper Ads

These video ads can appear in a variety of screen formats such as desktop, smartphones and TVs, tablets and more.

- Resolution: 640 by 360 or 480 by 360 / 19:9 or 4:3 ratio
- File size: a maximum 1 GB
- Frame rate: 30 FPS
- File format: MPEG-2, MPEG-4, H.264
- Audio codec: mp3, AAC

Ad type: Overlay Ads

These ads require one image or an animated image file that keep the animation loop under 10 seconds.

- Dimension: 480 by 70 Pixels
- File size: 150 KB
- File format: .png, .jpeg, .gif

Ad type: Sponsored cards

These ads need an image that clearly presents your product and a line for CTA.

- Dimension: 1:1 aspect ratio
- File size: maximum 2 MB
- File format: .png, .jpeg, .gif

How to Produce Perfect Creative YouTube Ads

One of the most important aspects of your YouTube advertising campaign is to create a video that provides exposure to your product or service it deserves. A strong video advert has the power to change your brand game in the industry. Of course, it should have its own voice as well. So before you start brainstorming ideas for your video ads, here are three questions you should always consider.

What value am I offering to my viewers?

What kind of videos would I and my audience watch all the way through?

What has no one ever seen before?

Within these answers, lies the secrets to crafting an amazing video that will serve its sale purpose.

Here is a checklist you will need to nail the creative of your video ad.

1. Make the first 5 to 8 seconds of your video advert engaging. After this point, the viewer decides if they want to continue watching the ad to the ad or just skip it.

2. Know the language, cinematography, and personality of the industry your brand belongs to and replicate these characteristics in your advertising so you can tailor video which your target audience wants to see.

3. Tell a story through your ad. Stories are one of the effective ways to engage your audience, but make sure it is supported with relevant information and fits within the advert time you have got.

4. Also, design a thumbnail for your video ad that fits its industry.

5. Focus on explaining one key point through your ad and avoid overwhelming your viewer.

Following are some additional tips that will keep your audience unable to rip their eyes off the ad.

6. Make valuable and unique content. These aspects will either make or break your video. Every time a viewer clicks on your ad, they are investing their attention and time to watch your video, and in return, you owe them something valuable. Because if your viewer doesn't feel like they are getting a good deal by watching your ad, they will never stick around. This doesn't mean you can simply represent or imitate video content from your top competitors to your competitor. It would be like presenting old wine in a new bottle, and this tactic never works. To truly win your viewers, you channel something else

that your viewer has never seen before, and that makes them feels different. Keep trying new things until you find something unique and interesting to present your viewers.

7. Honesty is the first priority. People get annoyed with misleading content, hiding behind captivating title, exaggerated thumbnails, and flashy buttons. You need to prove your brand reliability through your ad or something that is trustworthy to your viewers. Users can easily be piqued to check out your ad through headlines or thumbnails, but once they start watching your add and found worthless and not delivering the information that they were expecting, they will skip your ad.

8. Immediately spark advertisement through your ad. Your ad has a little time frame, and you have to utilize this space well to deliver your message and convince your viewer to take action as well. This can be achieved by grabbing your viewer interest

in the first 2% part of your video ad. Show something exciting or prove a point, rather than just stating. Avoid talking too much and give them a solid reason to make stick around until video ends. Once you succeed in assuring your viewer to watch your ad in the first few seconds, then your ad is a winner.

9. Tease your viewer. People crave closure, and that's why open loops and unanswered questions are used as marketing tactics to increase audience retention for the brand. At the beginning of your video, tease with a secret or incomplete information and specify that those who watch the video till the end will understand the whole story. Find something appealing in your video content, discuss a part of it in the beginning and save the rest of the information for later in the ad.

10. Set the tone with music and sound. Background music can make your video ad

enjoyable and memorable. Add music relating to the subject of the ad like motivational videos have inspiring sound, playful video ads have playful music or music with subliminal effect. Find a score for your ad that captures the mood you are hoping to hit. Don't use loud music that can overwhelm your viewer. For better results, adjust background music as you go such as escalate volume to increase energy or add silence for highlighting a new point.

How to Advertise on YouTube

If you are ready with your video ad, then you can go ahead and start with YouTube advertising.

Step # 1 – Create a YouTube Channel

Before starting an advertising campaign, it is best to upload your video to your YouTube account. To do this, log in to your YouTube account at https://www.youtube.com/ and then click "My channel" on the left side of the screen. If your channel is not created, you will be required to give the name of your YouTube channel. When you are done naming your channel, click "create channel."

Step # 2 – Upload Video on YouTube

Click on the small camera icon on the top right of screen and select upload video.

Then a new window will appear, drag or drop your video or select video file to upload and keep privacy set to public.

In the uploading video, fill out necessary information regarding the video like title, description, tags and more.

Step #3: Log into Google Ads Platform

Now, you can start creating your video advertising campaign for YouTube.

First, go to Google Ads at https://ads.google.com/home/ and sign in.

Step # 4 – Start the Campaign

On the main toolbar, click on campaigns, then click on "+" symbol and then + new campaign tabs.

Next, you will be present with different options as advertising goals. The options include sales, generating leads, driving website traffic, product and brand consideration, brand awareness and reach and promotion. Even if your advertising doesn't meet any of these options, you can select "create a campaign without goal's guidance" to build a campaign with your own goal.

After selecting your goal, scroll down to select your desired ad category. Since you are going for video content, therefore select video.

Scroll more towards the bottom of the page and check campaign subtype. Then click "continue."

Step # 5 – Configure the Campaign

In the new window, you will ask to name the campaign, stating budget, the time frame of the video ad campaign, the network to run the ad, languages, and language for the ad and bidding structure.

For best results, state the budget you can afford, better to start from low budget to test your ad strategy. You have a choice to set a budget for the daily or total campaign.

Also, bid high as YouTube is a competitive platform, the more the bid, the more likely views get to see your ad. Here, we have a choice to make from three out of five options.

Maximum CPV (cost per view) – the user is charged as per views received per ad.

Maximum CPM (cost per mille) – the user is charged for every thousand impressions on the ad.

Target CPM (cost per mille) – the user is charged for every thousand actions taken by clicking on the ad.

Networks decide where your ad will appear. There are three available options.

- YouTube search results
- YouTube videos
- Video partners on the display networks

It is best to uncheck "video partners on the display networks" because it doesn't give better results. Since you will run the ad on YouTube, so uncheck YouTube search result as well.

Select language and location (one or multiple) for your ad.

Scroll down to inventory type and leave it to standard. Click on the drop-down menu of exclusive content.

At the exclude types and label options, uncheck "content not yet labeled" check. Check embedded videos, live streaming videos, and games; these places have a busy audience so it will be wastage of money to run your advert here to grab attention.

Scroll more to write Ad group name.

In demographics, play around the options and uncheck unrequired gender, age group, and parental status.

Target your audience by entering keywords, it must relate to your ad and search terms used by your audience.

You can also target the audience with topics, check the topics related to the message of your video ad.

Placements will put your ad in front of other videos. Begin by searching with a word or phrase, then look through the options and check those YouTube channels, videos, websites, and apps where you want to bring your ad.

Put your bidding as per your bidding strategy.

In the "create your video ad" block, copy and paste your uploaded video URL in step 2.

When the video pops up and if you select an in-stream ad and you will see some options to the bottom of the page. Final URL will be your website landing page address where you want to drive your traffic like a sales page. Type your website address in the space of Display URL.

If you select a video discovery ad, you will be given the option of thumbnail, headline and description and name to the ad.

Check call-to-action and write an appropriate statement for it.

Scroll down to companion banner and select upload image which will appear on the right-hand side of your ad.

See the right side of the window to check your ad expected performance, based on all the working and selected made before for the ad.

To get the best result, bid high but keep your budget low or within your means.

To finish up, click "save and continue" and then "continue to campaign" tab. That's it; your YouTube advertising campaign is set to run.

Track for Your YouTube Ad Campaigns

Now that your YouTube ad campaign is up and running, you can check how it is performing. Though you can sign into the dashboard to analyze your ad performance, YouTube recommends linking your YouTube ad campaign to Google Ads to gather deeper performance insights of your ad.

Here are key metrics you need to keep your eyes on the Google dashboard.

- Impressions: number of users that were exposed to your ad.
- Views: number of users that watched your ad for 30 seconds or more.

- View rate: percentage of user who was shown the ad and viewed it.
- Cost per click: the spending on every click on your ad.
- Cost per view: the spending for each view.

Earned actions: number of people who liked your video, subscribed your YouTube channel or visited your website as a result of viewing of your ad.

Here are the instructions to link the YouTube ad campaign to Google Ads:

- Sign in to your YouTube channel and go to Creator Studio by clicking on channel icon in the upper right corner of the YouTube page.
- Click on channel option on the left side of the screen and then click "Advanced."
- Click "Link a Google Ads account" under the "Google Ads account linking" head.

- Follow the instructions, then click "Finish" and wait until the Google Ads account to approve the request.

If you noticed that your YouTube video ad isn't performing as you were expecting, the one you can do is to try to number of people who watch your video to 30 seconds or past this mark. Think about it if the viewer is engaged in watching video for 30 seconds or most, the viewer is hooked to your business. As a result, the viewers could be interested in viewing more video ads and your chance to collect more CTA will increase automatically. This ultimately boosts the return on investment (ROI) of your YouTube advertising campaign. You can quickly increase the view rate of your ad with

- A/B test of your video content
- Custom affinity audiences
- Campaign level setting
- Ninja management
- Behavior-based retargeting

Conclusion

Now that you have acquired knowledge to make you understand that how Facebook, Instagram, and YouTube can boost your business through social media advertising in 2019, I encourage you to take the plunge and plan your own social media advertising campaign.

If you are already doing so, then you have pretty much conquered the entire video advertising universe for your business. Just make sure to consider the mentioned best practices for each advertising platforms so that you can increase your conversions as well.

www.ingramcontent.com/pod-product-compliance
Lightning Source LLC
Chambersburg PA
CBHW030500210326
41597CB00013B/741